STEVE JENSEN

THE SHORTEST DISCIPLE

FROM THE LIBRARY OF
PASTOR KIEL

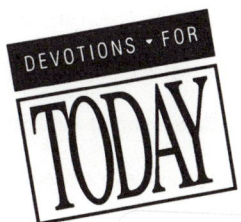

CRC Publications
Grand Rapids, Michigan

Cover and text illustrations: Paul Stoub

Copyright © 1993 CRC Publications, 2850 Kalamazoo Ave. SE, Grand Rapids, Michigan 49560

All rights reserved. With the exception of brief excerpts for review purposes, no part of this book may be reproduced in any manner whatsoever without written permission from the publisher. Printed in the United States of America on recycled paper. ♻

Library of Congress Cataloging-in-Publication Data
Jensen, Steve,
    The shortest disciple / Steve Jensen.
       p.   cm.
    Summary: A collection of forty devotions in which a young boy living at the time of Jesus joins his disciples and experiences his power first-hand.
    ISBN 1-56212-036-0
    1. Children—Prayer-books and devotions—English. 2. Christian life—Juvenile literature. [1. Prayer books and devotions. 2. Jesus Christ.] I. Title.
BV4870.J46 1993
242'.62—dc20   93-3902
                                                                                  CIP
                                                                                   AC

To Shirley, a writer gifted with the heart of an encourager.

CONTENTS

Preface 7
Follow Me 10
Jesus Forgives and Heals 12
An Unlikely Disciple 14
Learning How to Love 18
Do You Believe? 20
Who Is this Jesus? 22
Even the Spirits Obey 24
He Cares About Friends 26
School: Jesus' Style 28
Dinner Time! 32
Listen to Jesus 34
Who Is Number One? 36
Love Costs Something 39
What's Important? 42
You Gotta Ask! 44
Watch Your Heart 48
Even On the Sabbath 50
Thank You! 52
I Can See! 54
Never Too Short 57
Jesus Plans Ahead 60
Keep Looking Ahead 62
This Is God's House 64
The Biggest Gift of All 66
Not Everyone Loved Jesus 68
A Meal to Remember 70
Stay Awake! 72
Let God Do the Fighting 74
Hurting a Good Friend 76
Turn the Other Cheek 78

Jesus Is the Son of God	80
He Is Innocent!	82
He Is Guilty	86
A Helper from Africa	88
He Had to Die	90
The Curtain Falls	92
He Loved You, Peter	94
He's Alive!	96
He's In Heaven!	98
I've Got a Story to Tell	102

PREFACE

The first Christians told and retold the stories about Jesus Christ, what he said, how he acted, what he approved and what he disapproved, the kinds of people he healed, and the good news he proclaimed. Their teaching and worship centered in these stories about Jesus. He had become their Savior and Lord, and they wanted to know everything they could about him.

We can be sure that they told these stories not only to fellow adults but also to the children. And they must have told them in ways that helped the children love and respect Jesus and want to become his disciples.

In this devotional book for young children, the author has taken the gospel of Luke and retold its stories from the viewpoint of Jesse, a fictional thirteen-year-old beggar boy. Jesus lets him tag along with the disciples under Peter's care. So he shares in the greatest adventure of all, walking through the villages and hills of Galilee and Judea with the greatest teacher of all time.

Jesse's experiences and reactions will help your own children see Jesus as a truly living person as well as the majestic Son of God. They will come to know something of the grace and love of the Lord.

Steve Jensen, author of *The Shortest Disciple*, was born and raised in Japan to missionary parents and attended Japanese school through the third grade. He has served as Executive Director of Christian League for the Handicapped, an employment and outreach ministry for physically disabled adults. He is presently serving as Pastoral Assistant for Calvary Community Church, Williams Bay, Wisconsin.

We offer you this book with the prayer that you and your children will read it with enjoyment and spiritual profit.

> Harvey A. Smit
> Editor in chief
> Education Department
> CRC Publications

Dear Family,

The true story of Jesus is wonderful. Jesus came to earth as the Son of God and died for you and me. Before he died and rose from the dead, Jesus said and did many wonderful things. The story of Jesus' life is recorded in the Bible and it is all true.

The story in this book isn't a true story. And I'm not a real boy. It would have been fun to have lived at the time of Jesus and followed him on his trips. But not very many people could do that.

This story will help you think about what it might have been like to be a very young disciple. Read my story, then read each Bible passage—the true story. Enjoy my journey with Jesus as the Shortest Disciple.

Your friend, *Jesse*

MEDITATION 1
FOLLOW ME

My name is Jesse.

I grew up in a village next to the Sea of Galilee. Because we lived so close to the water, most of the people in our town fished for a living. But some were carpenters and farmers, too. In the center of our village, we had a fish market and a synagogue, which is like a church for Jewish people.

There isn't much to say about me. As a kid I was short and skinny and had long, stringy black hair. My clothes were always dirty. The village kids said I smelled bad. They called me names like "Pig" and "Dirtface."

Kids treated me that way because I was an orphan. I lived alone in an old boat on the beach, and every day I begged for money or food in the village. Each morning I would sit on the beach and wait for the fishermen to come in from their night on the sea.

On one of those mornings, my life changed forever. Just a little way from my boat a group of fishermen were cleaning their nets. They had fished all night and hadn't caught a thing. I knew some of the men; one was named Peter. He was the boss, and had a loud voice and big hands.

As I watched the tired men take care of the nets, I noticed someone coming from another direction. He was followed by a crowd of people. He stopped by the edge of the water. But people kept pushing closer and closer, forcing him to walk backwards into the lake.

"You there!" I heard him laugh to Peter. "I seem to be in a pickle here. Mind if I borrow one of your boats and push out from shore a bit? I need a place to stand and speak to these people."

"Fine with me, Rabbi," Peter answered. "I'm tired of working on these worthless nets anyway. We'll row you out." He turned to the other fishermen. "Take a break, men."

The fishermen pushed the boat toward the teacher, and he climbed in and sat down. I listened as he spoke. His words were unlike any I had ever heard before! He spoke all morning, then finally smiled and said, "Go home, everyone. My voice hurts from talking so much. And these kind fishermen need to get back to work."

The crowd slowly broke up. Then Jesus turned to the fishermen and told them to row out a bit and throw their nets in.

"But we've been out all night! There are no fish here," Peter said.

Peter obeyed the teacher anyway. And as soon as he did, the nets began to fill with fish. The men's muscles bulged as they pulled the nets in. Soon the boat was filled to the rim with huge fish. Water splashed into the boat as the fishermen began rowing toward shore.

I thought Peter and the others would celebrate, but no one said a word. The men were worried and scared. It was Peter who finally said to the teacher, "Leave me alone, Lord! I'm a sinful man!"

"Don't be afraid," the teacher said. "From now on, you'll be catching people for me."

Peter looked at the pile of fish and then at the teacher, who had begun walking away. Without saying a word, Peter left everything behind and followed. The others were stunned to see Peter walk away, but soon they followed too.

At that moment, I felt more alone than I had ever felt before. I looked at the village where I begged every day. I looked at the boat where I slept. Then I made my choice.

"Wait up!" I yelled, running after the group of men. Peter scowled at me as I approached them.

"What do you want?" he said.

"I want to come with you."

"But you're just a boy. Go back to your begging."

"But I want to come. I can help you! I know where to get food, and . . ."

Peter began to push me away, but the teacher stopped him.

"What is your name, son?"

"Jesse."

"Jesse," the teacher said, "the journey ahead is a long one. It won't always be as exciting as what you just saw. But I know you. You may come with us."

The teacher turned to Peter. "This boy is in your care now. Watch him like a little brother."

"But . . ." Peter started to argue.

"Peter," the teacher said, raising his hand to quiet him.

"Yes, Lord. Whatever you say."

Peter looked at me with a half frown/half smile and said, "C'mon kid. Let's go."

Read Luke 5:4-9

Lord, I'm like Peter. I don't always do what I should. But I want to follow you. I want to be your disciple. In your name, Amen.

MEDITATION 2

JESUS FORGIVES AND HEALS

"Get out of that seat!" the Pharisee grumbled at me. "We're here to listen to Rabbi Jesus, and we don't need the likes of you taking up space!"

The Pharisee had come with some other teachers. There was no room for them in the house, but others made space because the Pharisees were important people.

"It's O.K., Jesse. Why don't you go outside for a while?" Peter put his hand on my shoulder. "This man has come from far away. Give him your seat."

Peter's calm words and big hands moved me through the door before I could ask to stay.

Once outside, I saw crowds of people everywhere. They stood in the doorway and sat in the windows. Others sat on the steps leading to the roof.

I turned around to see four men staring at the house. Next to them on the ground lay a man on a stretcher. He could not move.

"Isaac, how do you think we're going to get our friend in there? Look at this crowd," one man said to another. "We'll never get through!"

"You're right," Isaac said. "It's too full. Let's forget it."

"No!" another protested. "We're not going back until Joseph here has been healed. I tell you, this Rabbi can do it. I've heard about him." The men continued arguing.

"The roof," I interrupted.

They still argued.

I spoke louder. "The roof! Take him up to the roof!"

The leader of the four men turned to me. "The roof?"

"Yes. Take him up to the roof and let him down into the room."

They laughed at first, but their faces soon changed.

"The boy is right, you know," one of the men said. "It could work! The roof is flat and made of mud tiles. We could dig away the tiles and lower Joseph right in front of the Rabbi. David, you've got rope in your boat, right?"

"Yeah sure. I'll get some."

"No—send the boy. While he's getting the rope, we'll take Joseph up to the roof. What's your name, son?" he asked, turning to me.

"Jesse."

"Jesse, do you know David's boat?"

"Yes," I said. I had often watched David row in from a night of fishing.

"Good. Run and bring back some rope. Make sure it's long enough to reach the floor."

I ran off before the man finished his sentence. "This is it!" I thought. "Now we'll see some excitement!"

The ropes were heavy, and by the time I returned, I was out of breath and sweating. So were the four men. They had carried their sick friend up the steps to the roof and had already removed the mud tiles.

David tied the ropes to the stretcher and the men lowered Joseph until the stretcher touched the floor.

"How dare you stop the rabbi while he's teaching!" the Pharisees yelled. Jesus ignored them.

"Friend," Jesus told Joseph, "your sins are forgiven. I've seen your faith and the faith of your friends."

The men on the roof were puzzled. Isaac whispered, "Isn't he going to heal our friend?"

The Pharisees began to grumble down below. I couldn't understand what they were saying, but Jesus quieted them and said, "I will show you that I can forgive sins by healing this man."

Jesus turned to Joseph. "Pick up your stretcher and go home."

Joseph looked at Jesus with hope in his eyes. He started to move a little bit. First he lifted one leg and then the other. He smiled as he sat up, and then he jumped right up off his mat with a happy yell!

I went to the edge of the roof to watch as Joseph ran through the door. Once outside, he leaped and threw his bed in the air. His friends dashed down from the roof and ran after Joseph, slapping him on the back.

I walked back to the hole in the roof and watched the excitement below.

"Jesus healed a man!"

"Jesus forgave his sins!"

"Praise God!"

Jesus looked up at me.

"See what faith can do?" he said.

Read Luke 5:17-26

Lord, please help my faith in you to be as strong as the ropes that held the man over the crowded room and as stubborn as the men who wanted their friend to see Jesus. In your name, Amen.

MEDITATION 3
AN UNLIKELY DISCIPLE

Although I didn't get along very well with the kids in my village, there was one thing about which we all agreed. We all hated Levi, the tax collector. He sat in a small hut by the side of the road, stopped people as they traveled, and forced them to pay money.

We enjoyed playing tricks on Levi. Sometimes we hid in the bushes and threw rocks at his booth. Most of the rocks fell short, but once in a while one of them would hit the side of the wooden shack with a bang! Levi would explode from his chair yelling and cursing, threatening to tax every kid's parents even more.

I can still remember the hot and lazy afternoon when we played our last practical joke on Levi. I had followed the gang of boys on the road past Levi's booth. We walked quietly, trying not to attract his attention. But one boy sneaked a glance at him.

"Hey guys!" the boy whispered excitedly. "He's asleep!"

We turned to see Levi, leaning back on his chair, fast asleep.

"Let's do something," one boy hissed.

"Like what?"

"I don't know. Throw something, maybe."

"Naah. That's boring. We always do that."

"What if we tip over his booth while he's still in it?" I whispered from the back of the crowd.

The argument stopped, and everyone looked at me.

"Hey," the leader laughed. "The orphan boy has an idea! Didn't think you had it in you, Dirtface."

His insult stung, but I felt proud of my idea. "Well, are we going to talk about it, or are we going to do it?" I said boldly.

The leader motioned with his hand. We were to split up into two groups and to surround the booth. Six of us crouched on each side, gripping the bottom of the booth. Levi was still snoring.

"Lift it slowly," said the leader. "We don't want to wake him until we're ready to tip it."

We leaned the booth back slowly at his command. When it began to tip on its own, the leader yelled out "Now!"

The booth tipped over on its side, knocking Levi flat against the wall with a yell.

We ran in all directions, too scared to look back but too excited not to laugh. We knew by Levi's cursing that he wasn't hurt.

"I'll tax the life out of your parents!" Levi yelled.

I caught my breath as I rounded the bend in the road and watched from behind a wall. Levi looked up the road to see if he could catch any of us, but we were too far away. He gave up and surveyed the booth laying on its side. Angrily he shook his head as he pushed the booth upright again.

As soon as I saw that our fun was over I looked around for the other boys, but they had all disappeared. Seeing that there was no one to share the excitement with, I decided to head back to the beach. But before I got out on the road, I saw Jesus walking toward Levi. I jumped back behind the wall to watch.

Jesus stopped to talk with Levi. I saw Jesus smile and motion "Follow me" with his hand.

And Levi did! He stepped out of the booth and followed Jesus.

As they came closer to where I hid, I heard Levi say, "Why don't you come to my house tonight? I'll have a banquet and invite my friends."

"That would be fine, Levi. I would love to come."

I couldn't believe my ears! Jesus was going to eat with a tax collector!

As the two passed by me, Jesus called out, "Let's go, Jesse. You can't hide all day. Levi has a feast to prepare, and he may need some help."

I had been caught! I wanted to run into the back streets, but I couldn't resist a command from Jesus any more than Levi could. I ran to Jesus and looked up at Levi timidly. My words came without thinking.

"I'm sorry, sir. I helped push over your booth. It was my idea."

Levi laughed. "That's all right, son, I deserved it," Levi said. "I was a lazy and cruel man. Your prank was well-timed. If you had not awakened me, I may have slept while Rabbi Jesus walked by. I should be thanking you."

We all laughed. Levi was not such a mean fellow after all. Jesus' command had changed him. He was a new man. He was a disciple.

Read Luke 5:27-32

Lord, don't let me think that other people could never follow you. You came to earth for unlovable people like Levi. And you came to earth for me. Thank you. Amen.

MEDITATION 4

LEARNING HOW TO LOVE

"Down the mountain, men!" Jesus called out. His cheery voice woke us up out of a sound sleep. "We've got people waiting who need to know about God's kingdom. Let's go!"

We quickly put on our sandals and gathered our things.

As we walked down the mountain, I saw what Jesus meant. Hundreds of people were walking up from the village toward us. They rushed at Jesus when they saw him. Sick, lame, and blind people cried out for joy as he healed them.

We had seen Jesus heal people before, but never so many at one time. People were healed just by touching him! It made me feel important to be a follower of such a powerful man. Other kids my age looked at me jealously.

"Do you think he could do something special, like make me taller?" a boy asked.

"He could if he wanted to," I said. "Maybe I'll ask him for you when I meet with him later," I bragged.

"What's he like, Jesse?" a girl asked. "Is he nice?"

"Yeah, he's nice to everybody." The more I talked, the more important I felt.

Then Jesus turned toward the disciples. "Sit down," he said.

"You've seen great things today, haven't you?" We all nodded and smiled. "Now I have something important to tell you while everyone else listens. You're happy because of what you see and because you're a part of all this. You feel special because you are my disciples. But let me tell you what's more important.

"Happy are you who know your need, for yours is the kingdom of God.

"Happy are you who hunger for the right things, for you will be satisfied.

"Happy are you when people hate you because of me."

As Jesus spoke, I began to understand that the things I thought were important were not important to Jesus. His idea of happiness was unlike anything I had ever heard. And then he said something that surprised me even more.

"Love your enemies, do good to those who hate you."

I was shocked. I had grown up being hated by everyone. The other kids—the same kids who were here listening today—hated me because I didn't have a mother or father. The people in town hated me because I begged for money. The Pharisees hated me because I was dirty. Now Jesus was asking me to love all of these people!

I looked at the kids I had bragged to just minutes before. They were listening closely to Jesus and didn't pay attention to me. I looked at each one and decided to obey Jesus.

"I love you, Aaron." I said quietly to myself. "I forgive you for taking my only coat and throwing it into the garbage dump."

"I love you, Esther. I forgive you for running through the streets yelling 'Jesse is a pig.'"

"I love you all!"

"What was that, Jesse?" The girl standing closest to me turned and stared. She must have heard me!

My face turned red. I knew I had to say out loud what I had thought in my heart if I was truly going to forgive.

"I love all of you and forgive you," I said. The other kids turned their attention from Jesus. Some understood and smiled, but others gave me funny looks and walked away, laughing. "Did you hear what he said? What a wimp!"

Two of the kids, a brother and a sister, stayed behind. The older sister said, "Don't listen to them, Jesse. I think the Rabbi's right. We're sorry we haven't shown love to you. Maybe you could come home with us. Maybe our parents will let you live with us."

"Thanks, but I'm going to stay with Jesus."

The two seemed disappointed, but they understood.

"Well, take care," the little brother said. "Will you ever come back here?"

"I don't know," I answered. "Jesus said we'd be in Capernaum a little while longer, but then we'll go to other villages and towns. One day, we'll go to Jerusalem."

We parted company as I followed Jesus and the disciples down the mountain.

I felt better. I had loved and forgiven the kids that hated me. And I knew that I was loved.

Read Luke 6:27-31

Lord, I need to learn how to love people I don't like. I sometimes need to learn how to love people that don't like me. Following you won't always be fun. Help me know that loving people is more important than the blessings you give. Amen.

MEDITATION 5
DO YOU BELIEVE?

Artemis was my friend. He was a slave who had been kind to me when I was younger. Before I started following Jesus, Artemis used to put leftover food on a window ledge at his master's house for me. His master was a wealthy and important man in our town, so the food was always good. Artemis said he'd be in big trouble if I ever got caught eating the food, but I told him not to worry. I knew the Centurion loved him.

So when I heard the town leaders ask Jesus to heal a Roman soldier's sick slave, I didn't want to believe that it could be my friend.

"Is it Artemis?" I asked as I tugged one leader's coat.

"How would I know what the slave's name is?" the grumpy man growled. "All I know is that he must be healed. The Centurion is a very important man in our village, and if this slave is important to him, then he's important to us. The rabbi *must* see him."

"Are you sure you don't know what the slave's name is?" I asked again.

"No, I don't. Now scram! I have to finish talking with the rabbi. Whoever this slave is, he's so sick that he could die any minute."

The other Jewish leaders pleaded with Jesus to visit the Centurion's slave. They wanted Jesus to go because the Centurion was good to the Jews—he even built their synagogue. He was also in charge of one hundred Roman soldiers, so the leaders wanted to make him happy, no matter what. I don't think they cared much about the slave.

I looked up at Jesus as he listened to the Jews. I didn't say anything, but I hoped he would see the fear in my eyes. I felt more and more certain that the dying slave was indeed my friend Artemis.

Jesus saw me and asked me to come with him to the Centurion's house.

"Is the slave's name Artemis?" I asked Jesus.

"Yes, it's Artemis. Do you know him?"

"Yes. He's my friend. He used to give me food. Can you heal him?" I pleaded.

"Do you believe I can, Jesse?"

"I think so."

I had seen Jesus heal many people before, but now I wasn't sure if he could heal Artemis. Healing strangers was one thing, but Artemis was my friend. Family and friends had been taken away from me before. Did it matter to Jesus how I felt? Did it matter to Jesus how Artemis felt? I wasn't sure if I really believed.

But there was no doubt that the Centurion believed.

"You don't need to go in," a friend of the Centurion told Jesus. "He won't come out of the house to meet you, because he doesn't feel special enough to do so. He said he knows that you can command that Artemis be healed from here."

My heart sank. Why would the Centurion do such a foolish thing? I felt sick at the thought of losing another friend.

The Centurion's friend continued. "The Centurion believes you can do this because he knows what it's like to give orders to people. He doesn't always need to be there. He only needs to pass the message along. Artemis will be healed if you just say the word."

Jesus laughed out loud. "Wow! This is incredible! Did you hear this?" he asked the people following him. "I've never met anyone with this much faith. I don't even know any Jews who have this much faith."

He turned to the Centurion's friends. "Go to the Centurion's house and tell him that I also give commands. His servant is healed."

"Really?" I asked Jesus as the men left.

"Really what, Jesse?" Jesus asked.

"Will he really be all right? I mean, you didn't touch him or anything. How do you know Artemis is OK?"

"Don't you believe I can heal people without touching them?"

"Yes, I believe, but I thought you might not want to heal him for some reason."

"Jesse, don't be afraid to want something enough to believe. The Centurion wanted Artemis to live, and he believed that I could heal him. And that was all I needed to know."

Read Luke 7:1-10

Lord, do I really trust you to be able to do anything? Please help me to trust you with things and people that are special to me. Amen.

MEDITATION 6

WHO IS THIS JESUS?

"Climb in, Jesse," Peter yelled as I stood next to the boat. We were headed across the lake with Jesus to Gerasene. I was nervous—I had lived under a boat for a long time, but I had never sailed in one.

"Don't be nervous, Jesse," Peter said calmly. "Sit up front there and you can watch for fish as we travel."

I climbed in and Andrew pushed us out into the lake.

"Watch your heads, you landlubbers!" Peter yelled to Levi and the others. The mast and sail swung around to catch the wind, and we were off, cutting through the waves.

I spent the next hour enjoying the sun's reflection as it danced like diamonds on the water. I saw several small schools of fish. But when I looked up at the sky again, I started to worry about our boat trip.

"Peter!" I yelled back. "There are some clouds up ahead."

"Don't worry, Jesse," Peter called. "They should blow off soon. But if it does storm, we'll be OK. Trust me, kid. I've done this hundreds of times."

Jesus was sleeping in the back of the boat. I was happy to see him rest; the last few weeks had been hectic. Everywhere we went he was asked to teach or heal. And when he wasn't doing that, he was praying.

I looked at the sky again. This time I felt a strong, wet wind hit my face. The diamonds that had earlier danced on the lake were gone. The sun was covered by dark clouds. I heard thunder in the distance.

"It's going to storm!" I yelled to Peter.

"I know," Peter answered. His confident look had disappeared. He seemed worried as he studied the oncoming storm. "It may be a big one," he said.

Peter was right. The storm was big. I crouched down in the front of the boat and looked back at the disciples.

The disciples took off their coats and pulled them up over their heads as it began to rain.

They crouched down like me to get as close to the bottom of the boat as possible. The sail swung wildly back and forth above them.

"Hold on for your life!" Peter yelled. "If the boat tips over, jump away from it and then swim back and hold on. Andrew, you take care of Jesse."

The storm raged stronger and louder. Lightning streaked wildly through the air. The thunder boomed. The waves pitched higher and broke over the side. Our boat, sitting low in the water with so many men, took on water quickly. Everyone bailed water out with their hands.

In the midst of the yelling and bailing, I looked toward the back of the boat.

Jesus was still sleeping.

"How in the world can he sleep?" I thought. Peter and the others had noticed the same thing.

Peter yelled, "Lord! We're sinking! Wake up!" His voice was lost in the raging storm, so the others joined him. "Wake up, master. We're sinking! We're going to drown!"

Jesus finally woke up, rubbing his eyes. The storm continued as strong as ever.

"Master, we're going to drown in the lake," Peter repeated.

Jesus said nothing. He stood up and spoke.

"Wind!" he commanded, "Stop this nonsense. And waves, be still. I'm trying to sleep, and these men are all in a panic because of your antics."

The lake and sky became still. There was no thunder, no rain, no lightning. The boat bobbed slightly in the calm water. We all stared at Jesus in shock.

"Where is your faith?" Jesus asked us.

No one answered him. How could we? Jesus sat down again and propped his pillow up to continue his nap.

"Who is this man?" John asked. "We know he's a rabbi and a special prophet from God. But to calm a storm with words? He just spoke to the storm as if . . ."

"As if he were God," Peter finished John's sentence.

We all looked at one another and then at Jesus.

Could it really be true?

Read Luke 8:22-25

Lord, you are God. You have control over the waves, the rain, the wind, and the thunder. Please have control over my life. Quiet me when I feel upset. Comfort me when I am afraid. I trust you to take me through life's journey. Amen.

MEDITATION 7
EVEN THE SPIRITS OBEY

Our boat arrived safely a couple of hours after the storm. We were all glad to stand on dry ground. We were glad, that is, until we saw what greeted us.

There in front of us stood a man with long, stringy hair and a dirty beard. He wasn't wearing any clothes. He stared at us with wild eyes, as if we had landed on his private property.

"What do you want with me, Jesus, Son of the Most High God?" he screamed. His voice was unlike any we had ever heard before. We all backed into the water, closer to the boat. But Jesus stood calmly in front of the man.

"I beg you!" the man screamed. "Don't torture me!"

"How could Jesus be torturing this man?" I wondered. I clung to John and peered from behind him. John was afraid too—he held tightly to the side of the boat. He called up to Peter who stood closer to Jesus. "Peter! Why is he crying out like that?" John asked.

"Jesus has commanded an evil spirit to come out of him," Peter said. "Come over here, John. It's all right."

John obeyed. Not wanting to lose the protection of John's coat, I followed.

"What is your name?" Jesus asked the man.

"Gang," the man said, "because there are many evil spirits living in me."

Suddenly, many terrible voices cried out from the man's mouth. "Don't send us to the dark! Please, Jesus, Son of the Most High God, we beg you!"

I tugged on John's coat. "Who's talking, John? Who are they?"

"They're evil spirits, Jesse. You can't see them. They control the man's mind and feelings so that he can't live a normal life. They're pleading with Jesus not to send them to a dark place where they would be kept as prisoners. They want to stay here on earth and use this man's body to get around."

"You mean like we use a boat?" I asked.

"Sort of," John said. He turned his attention from me to Jesus.

"Evil spirits," Jesus said, "you have ruined this man's life. Leave him. As you have begged of me, you may enter the bodies of those pigs over there."

Jesus pointed to a herd of pigs up on the hillside overlooking us. The pigs suddenly became excited, jumping around crazily. All at once they rushed down the hillside. Their awful squeals hurt my ears as they headed toward the lake and splashed in, disappearing under the waves.

It was awful to watch the animals drowning, but it was wonderful to see the man whom Jesus had just healed. He lay quietly at Jesus' feet.

"Jesse," Jesus called over to me. "Get this man a coat. And get a rag from the boat so we can wash him."

I ran back to the boat and picked up a coat and a rag. I dipped the rag in the lake and brought it to Jesus. He washed the man's face with one hand and combed back his hair with the other hand. The man was tired, but happy. He was well again. He smiled as he sat up and looked at Jesus.

"Let's go back, men," Jesus said. "We won't be wanted here."

As soon as Jesus said this, a large crowd of people ran down the hill. Several looked into the water where the pigs had jumped. Others ran toward us. "Get out of here! Leave us alone!" they cried. They looked as if they were afraid of what Jesus had done.

The disciples jumped into the boat. Jesus shook his head sadly and turned to leave.

The man who used to be called Gang spoke out. "Please, take me with you!" he cried.

"I would love to have you join us, but I need you to stay here," Jesus called. "Tell these people and others what God has done for you. A man is much more important than a herd of pigs. Tell them that, won't you?"

Read Luke 8:26-39

Lord, I sometimes don't understand the things in this world.
But I'll still follow you in times when I don't understand.
In your name, Amen.

MEDITATION 8

HE CARES ABOUT FRIENDS

Our trip back across the lake was quiet. James caught a fish. Thomas and Andrew played a game. I slept most of the way. When I awoke, I could see the shore in the distance and what looked like a large crowd waiting for us. "Peter," I called back. "Look at all those people!"

The rest of the disciples and Jesus sat up and looked. Seeing the crowd of happy faces made us feel welcome.

As we landed on shore, the old fisherman who had loaned us the boat came running. He was excited to see us.

"Peter! I can't believe it. You made it through the storm! We thought you had all drowned for sure!"

"There's plenty to tell you, old man. It was Jesus who saved us...." Peter was interrupted by a group of people pushing through the crowd, calling out to Jesus. They were led by an important-looking man.

"It's Jairus," I announced as the man approached. "He's a ruler at the synagogue."

Jairus dropped to the ground and knelt in front of Jesus.

"Rabbi, please come," he begged. "My daughter is dying. Save her, please."

I knew Jairus' daughter. Her name was Hannah. She was the one who overheard what I said to the kids while they listened to Jesus preach on the mountainside. I always thought she was special.

I didn't have to hear Jesus' answer; I already knew Jesus could heal her. "He might even heal her from here," I thought, "just like he healed Artemis."

Suddenly an idea hit me. "Wouldn't it be great if I could be in the room to see Hannah get better? Maybe I can get to her house and be the first to see the miracle."

I ran for Hannah's house as fast as I could and arrived there within minutes. Many of Jairus's friends and family stood quietly around the house. They were there to comfort Hannah's family.

I yelled through an open window. "Please let me in! I need to see Hannah!"

Hannah's mother answered, "I'm sorry, but Hannah is sick."

"I know, but I was just with Jesus. Your husband is with him now. Jesus is going to heal Hannah—I'm sure of it. Can I come in and see her? Please?"

"Well . . . all right. Come in, come in. Hannah is in the next room."

I made my way through the crowd and slowly opened Hannah's door.

She was lying on a cot in a corner. I walked in and left the door open. Hannah's mother followed me in.

"Hannah, are you all right?" I asked.

She didn't answer.

"Are you awake?" I touched her arm gently.

She was hot with fever. Her face was sweaty and her skin looked gray. She opened her eyes slowly.

"Jesse?" she asked.

"Yes, it's me. You're going to be all right—I'm sure of it. Jesus will heal you, and I'm going to watch it happen," I said to cheer her.

Her mother crouched next to the cot, and I stood back, waiting. Nothing happened. Each breath that Hannah took was heavier. Soon she stopped breathing completely. Her mother held her and wept.

"Jesus," I cried softly, "you were supposed to save her. Why did you help the crazy man in Gerasene and not Hannah? She didn't do anything wrong."

People stood quietly by the door as Jairus, Jesus, Peter, James, and John came into the courtyard.

"It's too late," Hannah's aunt told them. "She's dead." Jairus hurried to his wife's side.

"She isn't dead. She's sleeping," Jesus said as he walked over to the cot.

Jesus held her by the hand and commanded, "Hannah, get up!"

Hannah sat up in bed, opened her eyes, and smiled.

"You're alive!" I blurted out.

"Of course I'm alive. And I'm hungry."

"Give her something to eat," Jesus told Hannah's mother. "She's hungry."

Hannah's mother didn't move.

"Madam," Jesus said again, "please get the girl some food. She's hungry."

"Yes sir," Hannah's mother said. "Thank you. Thank you so much!"

Later, when we left the house, I thanked Jesus too. But I was curious. "What happened?" I asked Jesus. "I thought you were right behind me or that you'd save her from where you were."

"Plenty happened, Jesse. Ask some of the others. They'll tell you. But for now, let's go—I'm hungry. How about you?"

Read Luke 8:40-56

Lord, help me to see things the way you see them. Everyone thought Hannah was dead, but you knew better. Let me see that there's always hope. Show me that good things can happen, even when times are bad. Amen.

MEDITATION 9

SCHOOL: JESUS' STYLE

The disciples were getting ready to go on special trips. Each disciple had teamed up with another as a traveling companion.

"But where are you going and what will you be doing?" I asked.

"We're going out to do what the Rabbi has been doing," James answered.

"That's right, Jesse. We're going to march across the countryside preaching and healing," Peter said.

"But why can't *I* go?" I asked Jesus.

"There will be times when Peter won't be able to keep an eye on you because he'll be too busy preaching or fighting Satan's spirits. Besides, I want you to stay with me and fight another kind of battle," Jesus said.

"What battle is that?" I asked excitedly.

"Your battle with your studies," Jesus answered. "Peter tells me you've not been spending much time on your lessons."

My excitement disappeared. I groaned and lowered my head. Ever since we left Capernaum, different disciples had been teaching me. Andrew taught me how to read and write. Levi taught me how to count. James taught me about things in the water. John taught me about the history of Israel.

"I want to spend some time alone with you," Jesus said. "But first let me send these men on their way." He turned to the twelve.

"Listen to me. You're going to travel in my name. When you go, don't worry about the things you will need. Stay with people who welcome you. Leave those who don't. Make your life simple. Preach my message and heal the sick. Now go; I'll be watching for you."

The pairs of disciples left in different directions. They were excited, and some even ran for a short distance.

"So, Jesse," Jesus said, turning back to me. "Lesson time! Are you ready for some adventure?"

Lessons? Adventure? I was puzzled.

"Now the first lesson," Jesus said, "is botany."

"What?" I asked.

"Botany. That's the study of plants. Listen carefully. Do you see that tree? What kind is it?"

"That's easy. It's a fig tree."

"How do you know?"

"Because it has figs on it," I said.
"Good. Can you get figs from thornbushes?"
"No."
"Excellent. Now you know."
"Know what?"
"That you don't get figs from thornbushes."
I was still puzzled.
"I'm teaching you a lesson about life, Jesse. When you look at others, don't look at what they are like—their hair, their clothes, the way they talk. Look at how they live their lives. If they are good, you'll see good fruit like love and joy and peace. But enough botany. How about architecture?"

"What's that?" I asked. Lessons with Jesus were more interesting than with the other disciples.

"You know, building houses and palaces."
"Oh, sure."
"Let's go down to the stream."
We took off our sandals and walked into the water.
"First, build a house out of rocks on that boulder over there."
I followed his directions and made a tiny house out of different-sized rocks.
"Now, down here near the water, build a house out of sand on the water's edge."

I spent the next 15 minutes creating a beautiful sand palace. I built two bridges, put small branches around it for trees, and found pretty stones in the stream to decorate the outside.

"Which is better?" Jesus asked.
"The sand palace, of course." I said.
"Why?"
"Because the rock house is ugly. But the sand palace looks great."

"Let's be sure," Jesus said. He waded out into the stream and threw handfuls of water at the rock house.

"What do you have now?" he asked.

"A wet house," I said.

"Right."

Then he splashed water on the sand palace. Immediately the walls began to crumble.

"Now what do you have?" he asked.

"A mess," I answered.

"Exactly. Now you've learned your second lesson."

"And what's that?"

"Be sure to rely on things that last. Things that look nice may not last. Doing what I tell you is like building a house on the rock. Ignoring what I say will bring disaster.

I was really learning. "What's next, Jesus?"

"That's enough for now, Jesse. Tomorrow we'll study finance and zoology.

"What?"

"Money and animals," Jesus explained. "Now let's go get lunch."

What an interesting way to learn about life!

Read Luke 6:43-49

Lord, teach me to trust in your word. It'll last through anything. And teach me to look for good things in my life. If I'm your disciple, I want to see that your word is making a difference in my life.

MEDITATION 10

DINNER TIME!

"Jesse, wake up," Peter leaned over and whispered to me. Our campfire had died out, and it was still dark. "We need to leave before sunrise so the crowds don't follow us. Get up quickly. We're going to Bethsaida."

"Why?" I yawned.

"Because Jesus wants to talk with us alone about the trips we took without him. He wants to know what we learned." The other disciples and Jesus were standing by the side of the road waiting for Peter and me. I got up as quickly as I could and followed.

The thought of being alone with Jesus cheered everyone. But within an hour after we arrived in Bethsaida, the crowds came. People from Galilee had heard where we were headed and followed us. As they arrived in Bethsaida, they told others about Jesus, and soon the hillside was covered with people lining up to see him.

Jesus was patient. He healed the people who were sick. Then he taught everyone about how God saw things and how people could enter God's kingdom. He talked for hours, and no one moved.

"Peter," Bartholomew whispered as the afternoon passed. "This sermon has been going on forever, and we haven't eaten since this morning. See if you can get Jesus to take a break. There's no food up here, so everyone will have to go down the mountain before it gets too dark."

Peter hesitated, but he knew Bartholomew was right.

"Rabbi," Peter said. "I hate to interrupt, but these people will need to get down the mountain and eat soon. Can you send them away? Maybe you can continue your sermon tomorrow."

"You feed them," Jesus said.

"But Lord, we only have five loaves of bread and two dried fish left from our Capernaum trip. That's supposed to be our breakfast for tomorrow. We just don't have enough money to buy food for all these people."

Jesus nodded patiently. "You men go out and have all the people sit in groups of fifty or so. Jesse, go get our breakfast."

I ran back to our campsite and found the food. Then I carried it quickly back to Jesus.

While the disciples went out and organized the crowd into smaller groups, Jesus reached down and held up the bread and fish to the sky. "Thank you, Father, for providing this food and for bringing these people." And then he began to break the bread and the fish into pieces.

"Jesse," Jesus said, "go down the hillside and get the baskets the olive pickers left. Bring them to me."

I ran to the olive orchard below us and found a boy to help me on the way. I could see the leaves and the black, ripe olives. Just like Jesus said, there were big baskets underneath the trees.

"What do you think he'll do with these?" the boy asked.

"Fill 'em," I said.

"But I saw how much food he had. He doesn't need these."

"Just wait," I said. "You'll see." I said it as if I knew what would happen. But if I'd been honest, I'd have had to admit that I didn't know how Jesus would do it.

The boy and I were both surprised when we returned with the baskets. Jesus was still breaking pieces from the loaves and the fish. A huge pile of food lay on the ground in front of him.

"Peter," Jesus said. "Start filling these baskets and deliver the food to the groups. Make sure everyone has enough. Jesse, spread out the baskets so the disciples can fill them."

I just stood there, staring at the pile.

"Jesse," Peter shook me. "Listen to Jesus. We've got to get moving."

It took over an hour to deliver all the food. Levi counted the number of trips we made with each basket.

"Five thousand men!" Levi shouted.

"And don't forget the women and kids," I added.

The disciples and I stood with our mouths wide open.

"What are you looking at?" Jesus asked us.

"Well . . . it's just that . . . umm . . ." we stammered.

"There's one more thing you need to do," Jesus said.

"What's that?" several of us asked. We all expected another miracle. Jesus chuckled and said, "Clean up."

Read Luke 9:12-17

Lord, I don't always have much to offer you, but teach me that all you want is all of me. Use me however you will in your kingdom. Amen.

MEDITATION 11
LISTEN TO JESUS

The crowds that followed us grew bigger after Jesus fed the people on the mountainside. Jesus had healed many people. He had taught even more people. But when news spread that he had fed thousands of people, many people who heard imagined what someone with such power could do for them.

"I say he's Elijah," I heard one man arguing with some others. "Elijah did things like this man does. Remember the story of how the oil and flour never ran out for that widow and her son? I tell you, he's Elijah."

"But how can that be? Elijah's been gone for 900 years!"

"I tell you he's Elijah returned. And with his power we'll be able to break free of Rome and its taxes. We'll have our own king!"

The idea of Jesus as king sounded exciting. I ran to tell Peter.

"Peter," I asked, "is Jesus going to be a king?"

He thought for a moment. "Jesus would make a great king, wouldn't he?"

"I heard a man say Jesus was Elijah the prophet."

"He's not Elijah, Jesse. But I will say this much. I think he's the Messiah, the Savior of Israel, the one we've been waiting for."

"The *Messiah*? What does that mean?"

"Many years ago, the prophets told us to look for a savior who will rescue Israel from its enemies. This messiah will be a king and will rule over everyone."

Several days after this conversation, Jesus came up to Peter, James, and John.

"I'm going up the mountain to pray," he said. "Come with me."

I looked up at Peter. "Can I come?"

"I suppose," Peter said. "But remember, it won't be time to play."

We hiked for over two days up Mount Hermon. The scenery below was beautiful, but Jesus kept his eyes straight ahead. It was late afternoon when we stopped. "We'll pray here," Jesus said.

Although the disciples and I meant to pray, we were tired from our long hike. The warm breeze made us fall asleep.

We slept soundly until we heard voices. When we opened our eyes, we saw a bright light, even brighter than lightning! The light was shining from Jesus as he prayed. The voices came from two men standing near Jesus. Jesus called them by their names—Elijah and Moses.

"Elijah and Moses?" I exclaimed to Peter. "But I thought they were dead!"

"They are, Jesse. They must have come from heaven."

"What do we do?" James asked.

"Do? I don't know," Peter answered.

"We've got to say or do *something*," John said. "This is the chance of a lifetime! Imagine, talking to Elijah and Moses! Come on—say something, Peter."

"But what do I say?"

James and John shrugged their shoulders.

"Honestly," Peter said. "I'm always the one who has to take care of things. You'd think I was your mother." He got up and approached Jesus and the two visitors.

"Ah, excuse me, Jesus. Why don't James, John, and I make some shelters, one for each of you. That way you can talk privately without anyone bothering you. And the shelters will keep the bright light from attracting people from the valley below."

Peter didn't have to worry about the light. Within moments, a cloud came down and covered all of us. Suddenly, a voice rang out.

"This is my Son whom I have chosen. Listen to him."

And then there was silence. When the cloud disappeared, so did Moses, Elijah, and the bright light. Jesus stood alone.

We stared at Jesus without speaking a word. We knew we had just heard the voice of God.

I always knew Jesus was special, but this was amazing. Jesus was God's Son! I was following the Son of God!

Read Luke 9:28-36

Lord, teach me to listen carefully to everything you say. There are a lot of people at school or on TV that want me to listen to them. But you're God. You're the most important person I should listen to. Amen.

MEDITATION 12
WHO IS NUMBER ONE?

The other disciples didn't believe we had gone up the mountain just to pray. They could tell there was something different about us, but we had promised Jesus not to tell what we had seen and heard. The other disciples were jealous.

Peter, James, and John didn't help matters. They didn't tell anyone what they saw, but they bragged that they would probably get special treatment from Jesus.

"We'll probably rule with him in his kingdom," James said.

"I think it'll be great," John added. "You guys can trust us three. Just let us know what you want and we'll talk to Jesus about it."

A few of the disciples mumbled quietly. But Levi spoke up. He thought it was unfair that Peter, James, and John thought they'd be special.

"I say we'll all be in charge equally," Levi argued. "If you three were to be in charge, Jesus would have said something by now."

"Nice idea, Levi," said Peter. "But who went up the hill with him? Don't forget he asked for us especially. He wanted to pray with us. I didn't hear him ask you."

"No. But what did you do up there?" Andrew argued. "Jesse told us you all slept. We did as much down here! You're no better than we are."

"Yeah, but who did he ask to follow him first?" James replied. "Remember, we let him use our boat, and he caught all those fish. The first ones asked are usually the most important. Jesse, you were there. We were first, weren't we?"

I looked at James and the other disciples. I was about to answer when I felt Jesus' hand on my shoulder.

"Gentlemen," he said, "do you see this young boy? Whoever accepts this boy just the way he is accepts me. And whoever accepts me accepts God.

"Do you want to know which one of you is more important? I'll tell you. The least important person among you is the one who will be the greatest. Jesse here might as well be the greatest. He's small and weak and shy. He knows there's no point in trying to be first. So stop arguing and work together."

The disciples were embarrassed about their argument. I was embarrassed because I, too, had felt special that Jesus had taken me up the mountain.

John broke the silence. "Lord, we're sorry for arguing about which of us will be greatest. But surely all of us will be greater than those who don't travel with you—like the man we saw driving out evil spirits in your name the other day. He's not one of us twelve, so he couldn't be among the greatest, right? We tried to stop him because he wasn't one of us."

"Don't stop him," Jesus said. "Listen carefully—that man accepts me. And remember, if he accepts me, he accepts God the Father. He accepts me because he isn't against me. He wants the same thing that I want. He just doesn't care whether or not he gets to be famous by following me all over the countryside."

Jesus was a little angry with John and the others. They still didn't seem to understand.

"Listen," Jesus continued. "The time is coming when we'll go to Jerusalem for the last time. Remember what I told you. You will someday choose whether you are for me or against me. Choose me like Jesse chose me, and you will be great. Nothing else that happens in Jerusalem will make you great."

Read Luke 9:46-48

Lord, teach me to put other people first. It's hard to do that when others can be selfish. And sometimes it feels so good to be first. But teach me to serve others as I follow you. Amen.

MEDITATION 13
LOVE COSTS SOMETHING

Jesus told stories that made his teaching special. One of his stories was about a Samaritan man. Jewish people hated Samaritans, but the Samaritan in this story was the hero. He showed love to a Jewish man who had been beaten by robbers.

The lesson was simple to understand. All people are our neighbors, and we need to love each one. I felt good that I understood the story. But it took me several days before I did anything about what I learned.

Jesus entered the synagogue one day with his disciples to study and to talk with other rabbis. I decided to go to the market instead. Reading old books wasn't my idea of fun.

"Come back before the sun is high in the sky," Peter said. "Don't get lost. We're heading for the village of Bethany after we have our noon meal."

"Don't worry about me, Peter. I'll be back in time."

I headed down the street toward the market with a coin Levi had given me. It was the first time I can remember holding money in my hand that I didn't beg for. And I knew what I would buy with the coin—a set of marbles. The marbles were made of beautiful stones shaved round and smooth as a fish's eye.

My heart raced as I got closer to the market. I could see fabric dealers waving their materials in the wind. Vegetable sellers held cucumbers in the air. A potter banged a clay pot with a stick.

A camel moved from its place along the side of a building, and then I saw him—the seller of games and toys! I ran toward him, clutching the coin in my hand. "Finally, my own marbles!" I cheered to myself.

"Please, help!"

I stopped in my tracks at the voice. I looked around and saw an old man huddled in the entryway of a building. His body was covered with old rags. Flies flew around his face.

"I'm blind," he called out. "Please spare me a coin, kind sir. I have no one to care for me. My sons and daughter are gone. My wife is dead. Please spare me a coin that I might eat."

I tried to escape on tiptoe.

"Please, sir, a coin!" the man insisted.

I gripped my coin tighter and stopped. "Doesn't this old man know this is the only coin I've ever had that didn't come from

begging? Doesn't he know I've never owned a bright, shiny marble in my entire life?"

"Please, sir. Answer me. Have pity on me!"

I looked ahead at the market, and then back at the old man. I felt angry inside; I really wanted those marbles. But I felt sad, too, because I knew what it was like to beg for food.

So I turned and walked toward the man. He heard my steps get closer.

"Ah, thank you, kind sir. Bless you. May the God of Abraham bless you and your family."

I stood over him. His eyes stared blankly. I took his hand in mine and placed the coin in it. At the touch of my soft, small hand, the man jerked his head up and grabbed my arm.

"You're just a boy!" he said. "Why are you giving an old man your money? Surely this isn't yours to give. Your papa's money no doubt."

"I don't have a father."

"Aaah. Your mother's then. She sent you to buy food in the market, eh? No, boy. I can't take your money. It is not yours to give."

"But it *is* my money, sir. And I choose to give it to you. I used to be a beggar too. You keep it."

I gently pulled my arm away from the man and turned back to the street.

"What is your name?" he asked.

"Jesse."

"Bless you, Jesse. May God bless you for your kindness."

Deep inside I knew God had blessed me, and not just because the man felt better. It was because I had done what Jesus would have wanted me to do.

Read Luke 10:25-37

Lord, what do I have that you want me to give up? Is there someone who needs my help? Is there someone who needs my friendship? Teach me to go out of my way to love those who need love. In your name, Amen.

MEDITATION 14

WHAT'S IMPORTANT?

"Please, Jesus. Come inside and eat with us," Martha said. Even from the street we could smell the wonderful food she was cooking.

"Martha, it's wonderful to see you again. Where is Mary?" Jesus asked.

A younger woman came to the doorway. She smiled and then ran to Jesus and hugged him. The rest of us couldn't wait to get inside. We were all tired and hungry from our travels, and the thought of Martha's home-cooked meal made our mouths water.

I ran ahead of the others toward the door. I just had to see all that delicious food!

"Jesse! Hold on boy!" Peter called out. "Don't be rude."

"But she invited us in," I said.

"Let the boy go, Peter," Mary laughed. "He looks like he could use a good meal."

The house was small. It had a room for sitting and eating and a kitchen. A stairway led to the sleeping rooms above. It wasn't a fancy place, but I liked it. It felt like a home.

"May we stay here forever?" I asked out loud.

Peter's mouth dropped open. "Jesse!" he scolded. The others laughed, including Martha.

"But it's a wonderful place," I said. "The village is quiet, and the people are so nice here." I looked at Mary and Martha.

"Of course you may stay here, my little prince," Mary said. "Our brother Lazarus would be delighted if all of you would stay."

"Where is your brother?" John asked.

"He's in the fields right now, but he'll be home for supper. Until then, please sit. I want to listen to Jesus," Mary said.

Jesus sat down on a couch, and Mary sat at his feet. The disciples gathered around in a circle. I stood in the doorway between the kitchen and the sitting room. Martha was in the kitchen preparing food.

Jesus spoke of many things. He explained our journeys to Mary and his reason for coming. Mary sat quietly and listened carefully to every word.

Meanwhile, the noise behind me in the kitchen grew louder. I heard the sounds of clay pots clattering, knives scraping, and vegetables being chopped loudly. I turned to see Martha staring at the doorway where I stood. As she worked, she mumbled with a frown.

"It's always been this way," she spoke out loud to no one in particular. "I do all the work around here, and pretty little Mary goes on as if the world ran all by itself without our help. All my life I've taken care of her, and now that we have the Rabbi and all these guests, what does she do? She leaves me here to do all the work."

Martha carried on like this for quite some time. But when she heard Mary's soft, high-pitched laugh come from the other room, she threw down her knife. She entered the room and coughed for attention. The disciples and Jesus looked up at her.

"Please, Jesus. Don't you care that my sister has left me to do the work by myself? Tell her to help me." Her voice was soft, but we could tell she was angry.

Mary got the hint. She got up quickly and headed for the kitchen.

"Martha, Martha," Jesus said. "You are worried about many things. Taking care of a house, a brother, and a sister is hard work, but there's really only one thing you need to do. And that one thing is what Mary chose to do. She chose to spend time with me."

Martha opened her mouth as if to protest, but Jesus stopped her. "Let her stay. And you come and join us too. We already know your hospitality and food is the finest in the land. So come and enjoy. Take off your apron."

Martha relaxed a little and smiled. Mary went back and sat at Jesus' feet.

"Jesse, you sit, too. You've been skipping too many of my talks lately. If you're going to be a disciple, you have to learn to listen and not just work or play. So sit still. I've got a story to tell."

Read Luke 10:38-42

Lord, I can do many things for you as a disciple. But sometimes you just want to spend time talking with me. Help me to remember to spend time reading the Bible and enjoying your company. Amen.

MEDITATION 15

YOU GOTTA ASK!

"I wish I could pray like Jesus," I said one day to the disciples. "His prayers are special. They're not just a bunch of words he has learned to repeat. They're real."

"I've thought often about that too," said Peter. "It's probably his prayers that allow him to do so much. Why, if I could pray like him . . ."

"So why don't we ask him to teach us?" John asked. He stood up and walked over to Jesus, who was sitting on a rock.

"Ah, Rabbi?"

"Yes, John. What is it?"

"We've been with you for quite a while now. And we've watched you praying quite often. We pray, too. But it seems your prayers are special."

"So you want me to teach you how to pray?" Jesus asked.

"Yes. John the Baptist taught his disciples to pray. We just thought that—well, you know—we ought to have our own special prayer too."

"Very well. Listen, all of you," Jesus said.

"When you pray, say: 'Our Father in heaven, hallowed be your name. Your kingdom come and your will be done on earth as it is in heaven. Give us this day our daily bread and forgive us our sins as we forgive those who sin against us. And lead us not into temptation but deliver us from evil.'" Jesus stopped and looked at John and the others.

"Does that give you an idea of what a conversation with God ought to be like? Do you have any more questions?"

I blurted out my question first. "Do you really mean that if we ask for something God will give it to us?" I asked.

"Yes, Jesse. As long as you ask God for things you truly need or things God wants you to have."

Jesus looked at his disciples. "You don't believe me, do you? Let me explain."

Jesus told us a parable about a man getting what he asked for, just because he was bold enough to ask. "Ask and it will be given you," Jesus said. Still, the disciples didn't seem convinced.

A little while later, Jesus took me aside.

"Jesse, will you do me a favor?"

"Sure."

"I want to teach the others what I meant about asking God for the things we need. And I have a plan." Jesus motioned for me to get closer. He whispered in my ear.

"Really?" I grinned.

"Yes. We'll try it tonight."

Jesus woke me in the middle of the night.

"It's time, Jesse. Go ahead with our plan."

I took off my blanket and walked over to Peter.

"Peter!" I yelled. "I'm hungry. Wake up!"

Peter snored.

"Please, Peter." I shook him. "I'm hungry. I want some food."

The other disciples were awake by this time. Peter blinked his eyes in the moonlight and propped himself up on one arm.

"Why in the world would you want bread in the middle of the night?" he whined.

"Because I'm hungry."

"Can't you wait till breakfast?"

"No, Peter. I'm *starved*!"

Peter tried to convince me to go back to bed, but I refused.

"Oh, all right," he finally said as he reached into his bag, mumbling to himself. He took out a small loaf of bread.

"There. Satisfied?"

"Yes. Thank you."

Suddenly we heard clapping at the opposite side of our circle.

"Well done! Well done!" called Jesus.

"Now do you get the picture?" he asked the disciples. "Do you understand now what I meant about boldly asking my Father? Ask, gentlemen, you must ask!"

The disciples laughed. Peter grabbed me and playfully wrestled me to the ground.

"You rascal, you! You were in on this all along, weren't you?"

I giggled at Peter. "Yes. And I bet you'll never forget to ask, will you?"

"I suppose you're right. Ask and you shall receive. OK, then, get to bed. No bread for you till morning." Peter took the loaf from my hand and went back to bed.

I wrapped my blanket around me and closed my eyes. "Ask and it will be given to you." Jesus' words were sometimes hard to believe. But I would never forget them.

Read Luke 11: 1-8

Lord, a lot of people know how to pray really well. I don't always pray well, but you don't care about that. You want me to ask you into my life. You want me to ask you for things as if I were a child. Lord, I am a child. Hear my prayers. In your name, Amen.

MEDITATION 16
WATCH YOUR HEART

Not all of our days with Jesus were happy. Some people in the crowds became angry with Jesus and accused him of being against God. I couldn't believe that people would accuse our kind master of such a thing. Peter was not surprised, though.

"Listen, Jesse," he said. "Do you remember the Pharisees when you were younger? Did you ever see them help the likes of you, an orphan boy?"

"No."

"Did you ever see them say a kind word to a dog or cat?"

"No."

"Did you ever see them smile?"

"No."

"There you have it. Don't be upset by what they say about Jesus. They're angry because of what he has said about them. And I suspect he'll tell them more things they don't want to hear. In fact, we're going to a Pharisee's house tonight, and there will probably be trouble."

"But why do we have to go? If Jesus doesn't like the Pharisees, why does he spend time with them?"

"I suppose it's because they're people, too. But enough talk," Peter said. "Let's get ready to go."

When we arrived at the Pharisee's house, Jesus laid down on the pillows next to the table and began to eat the meal prepared for him. He started out with a drink of wine mixed with honey. But before he was able to take a second sip, the host said out loud, "Rabbi, how can you eat without washing your hands, as is our custom?"

The whole room became silent.

I had never been at a fancy dinner before, but I knew something of what usually happened at these occasions. You see, the host of the dinner was supposed to have servants wash the feet and pour water over the hands of each guest. Jesus' feet had been washed, but no one had offered him water for his hands.

"You foolish men," he said. "You care more about what the outside of your life looks like than about what is going on in your heart. You love to practice rituals like washing your hands, but you don't love God."

Then a teacher of the law got upset with Jesus.

"When you insult the Pharisees, you're insulting us too," he said.

"You're right," Jesus replied, "I am. You're no better than the Pharisees. You give people all kinds of rules to keep, but you don't help them. Instead of teaching people, you keep them from knowing the truth."

The room was quiet. I didn't want to be there, and neither did Peter. The Pharisees and teachers of the law were angry about what Jesus had said. And Jesus was angry with them. Nobody moved except the servants, who walked around the tables trying to lighten the mood with more food and wine.

Jesus made the first move. "Come, Peter and Jesse. We're going."

I knew there would be trouble from that day on. The Pharisees and teachers of the law were upset. They were jealous of Jesus because the people liked his teaching. And they were upset because he told the truth about them.

I followed closely behind Jesus on our way back to Mary and Martha's house. He was looking at the people in the streets. He wasn't angry; he was sad.

"Do you know why I was upset, Jesse?" Jesus asked.

"Not really. I mean, I know the Pharisees are mean sometimes, but I'm not sure why you're so angry with them."

Jesus stopped in the middle of the road and held my hands, bending down so that his eyes were looking straight into mine.

"I'm sad and I'm angry because our Father never intended for people to act like the people in that room. Never, Jesse, never grow up to let your heart become cold and empty like theirs. Never let it say one thing and do another. Let it be true and kind and loving. Let it be real. Do you understand, Jesse?"

"Yes, Jesus," I said. "I do."

I meant what I said that day. And since that day, every time I wash my hands I remember Jesus' words.

Read Luke 11:37-54

Lord, protect my heart so that it will always smile. Help me to always have a kind word for a cat or a dog, and to always help people who need you. Let me be a true disciple and not a fake. Amen.

MEDITATION 17

EVEN ON THE SABBATH

One night, while we were sitting around a fire, I complained to Peter. "The most important people in the towns are all upset with Jesus. I've heard them talking. They don't like him. Can't you ask Jesus to stop saying things that make them angry?"

"I don't think so," Peter replied. "He says those things because he has to, Jesse. And Jesus is right about the things he teaches, even if they do upset people. Our job is to follow him."

I looked into the hot coals of the fire and pulled my blanket closer around me.

"Do you want to go back to Capernaum, Jesse?" Peter asked.

"No, I'll stay," I said. "It's worth it."

The next day was Saturday, the Sabbath. The Sabbath was the Jewish day of rest. We headed to the nearest synagogue, where Jesus had been asked to teach again. All the men were in the main room. All the women and children were up in the balcony or standing outside.

I sat on one of the stairs leading up to the balcony. At the bottom of the stairs was an old-looking woman whose back was bent over. Her face almost touched the stairs as she climbed.

I tiptoed down the stairs toward the woman. "Would you like some help?" I whispered. When she looked up at me, I was shocked. She was not an old woman. She was young! Her hair shone like black silk. There were very few wrinkles on her face, and her teeth were pearly white.

"Thank you, yes," she said softly.

I held one of her arms to steady her as she climbed. We arrived at the balcony and I led her to a seat, chasing away two little girls who sat at the end. No sooner had I seated her than Jesus' voice rang out.

"Woman, come here," he said as he looked up at us.

All the people in the synagogue gasped and whispered to each other. "What is he doing?" I heard one woman say. "Women aren't allowed to enter the main room." Others on the floor and in the balcony whispered with excitement. "Why does he want the woman to come forward? What has she done?"

"Maybe he'll heal her," said one boy.

His mother scolded him. "Nonsense. This is the Sabbath. Rabbis don't do such things on the Sabbath."

During the commotion I led the woman back down the stairs as quickly as I could. We stopped in the center of the main room and Jesus walked forward to meet us.

He placed his hand on her back and said quietly, "Woman, you are free now from your illness."

The woman immediately stood up straight. She was taller than I had imagined she'd be. Her long black hair fell down in straight rows to her waist. Her face lit up like a child's.

"Hallelujah!" she cried out. "Praise be to God!" Tears flowed freely down her cheeks as she danced for joy.

"Stop!" the ruler of the synagogue cried out from the side of the room. "What do you think you're doing, woman? This is the Sabbath. You know healing on the Sabbath is not allowed. How dare you interrupt the rabbi?"

"But he called me," she said. "And he healed me. I was bent over for so many years, and now . . ."

Jesus gently smiled and held up his hand to quiet the woman. "Please, you need not feel accused. You've done no wrong. Go, and continue your praise to God."

The woman left the room, and Jesus turned to the ruler of the synagogue. Jesus' smile disappeared, and anger flashed across his face.

"You hypocrite!" he cried out. "Even you will untie your oxen and donkeys to give them a drink on the Sabbath. Why then shouldn't this woman be healed on the Sabbath? She was bent over for eighteen years! You care more about your animals than you do about people."

The man and his friends didn't say anything. I could see that they knew Jesus was right. They looked down at the floor and shuffled their feet, mumbling to themselves.

The people in the synagogue cheered, and their excited whispers continued for many minutes. It was a happy Sabbath for all the people there.

I realized then that Peter was right. Jesus was doing the right thing. And I wanted always to be at his side.

Read Luke 13:10-17

Dear Jesus, I thank you for your wonderful power to heal. Help me to see what's really important to you, every day of the week. Amen.

MEDITATION 18

THANK YOU!

"We're going to Jerusalem, Jesse!" Peter called out.

I jumped out of the tree where I had been picking olives. "Jerusalem?" I asked excitedly. "Do you really mean it?"

"Yes, we're leaving now. Hurry. Get your coat and stick. Wash your face before we go, and clean up—you've got cobwebs all over you."

Our trip took several days. One day as I ran ahead of the group, I saw several people sitting around a campfire. They wore ragged clothes and were huddled closely together. I approached them quietly from behind.

"Hello," I said. "We're on our way to Jerusalem."

The men jumped up at my greeting and spun around to look at me.

"Get away, boy!" one yelled. "Don't ever sneak up on us like that again."

I was shocked by his harsh voice, but I was even more stunned when I saw their faces. Under their ragged clothing and large scarves were faces I will never forget. Large sores covered their bodies. Their lips and feet were swollen.

"We have leprosy, boy! Get away from us or you'll get it too."

"Get away from here!" another man yelled. He picked up a stick from the fire and headed toward me.

"Wait! I know someone who can help you," I said without thinking.

"Help us? How?" the man with the stick asked.

"He can heal you," I stammered.

A couple of the men laughed. One yelled at me. "Go on with you. Don't tease us. We've had enough of you kids taunting us and throwing rocks at us. Leave us alone."

"But Jesus is coming this way. He's healed many people before. Honest!"

The men were silent. They looked at one another.

"You know," said one, "I've heard other travelers speak of this Jesus. They tell the same stories as this boy."

"Are you sure it's the same Jesus, son?" one asked.

"Yes, I'm sure. I'm one of his disciples."

"Then go and ask your master if he will come and heal us."

I turned and ran back to where I had left Jesus. He had finished teaching and was approaching the village. Just as I reached him I heard a shout from behind me.

"Jesus, Master, have pity on us!"

Jesus raised his hand as he walked toward the men. "Go show yourselves to the priest. Show them that you are healed."

The men turned back to the village as Jesus commanded.

"But are they really healed?" I asked. "Just look at them. They still look terrible."

"They will be healed because they're trusting that what I say is true."

We watched as the ten lepers approached the village. We could see each one stop and look at himself and then at the others. Realizing they had been healed, they leaped into the air. They hugged each other. They threw off their dirty rags and danced in circles.

All ten of the lepers started to run into the village, but one of them stopped short. He turned on his heel and ran straight toward us. When he reached us, he threw himself on the ground and panted, "Thank you, Master! Thank you, Jesus! Praise be to God—I'm healed!"

The man took off his coat and rags. His skin was clean and whole.

"You're a Samaritan!" Judas cried.

"Yes, I am," the man answered. "I know you Jews hate my people, and you don't like talking to us. But I couldn't go into the village without coming back to thank Jesus. Praise be to the God of Abraham!"

"I healed ten men. Where are the other nine?" Jesus asked. "Why were you the only one to return to thank me? Get up. Your trust in me made you well."

The man got up and bowed again to Jesus, then turned to me with a smile.

"Thank you, young man, for telling us about Jesus. We would have hidden behind the bushes if you had not told us about him."

I smiled and touched the man's arm. He pulled away for a moment, then realized that he was no longer a leper. He reached for my hand.

"Thank you, son. Thank you."

Read Luke 17:11-19

Lord, I don't want to be ungrateful by forgetting to thank you. You've done so much for me and my family. Thank you for dying on the cross to pay for my sins. Thank you for letting me go to heaven someday. Amen.

MEDITATION 19
I CAN SEE!

"The road is so crowded, Peter. Why is that?" I asked as we got closer to Jerusalem.

"Because soon it will be Passover. And because news of Jesus' work is spreading."

"Can I run up ahead to tell people in the other villages that Jesus is coming?" I asked.

"No. Stay close beside me. Don't run up ahead. This road isn't safe. There's no telling what thieves might be hidden along the way. And we have to keep an eye on Jesus, too," Peter added.

"Why?" I asked.

"Don't you remember what Jesus said yesterday? He told us that he was going to be captured and killed by the Gentiles."

"But how does he know that?"

"I don't know. The others and I talked about it. The only thing we can figure out is that some thieves or a murderer will go after him. So we're all staying close to Jesus. The more men we have to protect him the better."

"But if Jesus said it was going to happen, you can't stop it from happening, can you?" I asked further.

Peter stopped and looked down at me.

"Listen. I don't understand everything he says. No one does. All I know is that Jesus is the Messiah and he's here to save his people. Now if some thief is going to try to end all that, then I'm not going to let it happen."

John interrupted. "Peter, don't get the boy all upset. After all, we really don't know that it's going to happen. Maybe Jesus meant that he'd be arrested instead of killed. Then he'd just have to sit in a jail for a few days. He wouldn't be the first prophet to have to do that, you know."

Just then we heard a loud shout: "Jesus, son of David, have mercy upon me!"

We froze in our tracks. In the distance we saw a man by the side of the road raising his hands in the air. Several travelers stood by him and yelled at him to be quiet. But he didn't stop.

"Jesus! Jesus!"

"Bring the man here, Andrew," Jesus said.

"I'll go with you, Andrew," Peter added.

I followed them both.

"We've got to be careful, Andrew," Peter said. "This may be a trick to get Jesus. Don't trust anyone around here. We don't know anything about this fellow or about the people standing around him."

Peter asked the questions when we came to the man who had shouted.

"What's the problem?" Peter asked sternly.

"I'm blind and I want to see Jesus."

"What's your name?"

"Bartimaeus."

"Where are you from?"

"Jericho. I came out here to beg."

"Do you know any of the people who are standing around you?"

"No."

Peter turned to look at the people. They shook their heads. "We're from Galilee like you," they said.

"All right, old man. Guess you can't do much harm. Jesse, take this man to Jesus."

The beggar got up to follow. He was skinny and covered with dirt.

"This way, sir. Jesus is not far from here," I directed.

Peter and Andrew followed closely behind us.

"How did you become blind?" I asked Bartimaeus.

"I don't know. Each day that I woke up I could see less and less. One morning everything was just white."

Jesus met us on the road.

"What do you want me to do for you?" Jesus asked.

"Lord, I want to see."

"Then receive your sight. Your faith has healed you."

"Ah!" Bartimaeus cried out. "I can see! I can see! Look there—a tree by the road! And here's an ant on the ground! I can see! I can see! Praise God!"

Bartimaeus began leaping in the air. I thought his skinny bones would break!

"Let's go," Jesus said to the disciples. "We have to get to Jerusalem."

"May I come too?" Bartimaeus asked.

"Sure. Join us if you wish."

Bartimaeus fell in behind our group. He talked happily to the crowd. Every once in a while he stopped to look at a tree or a flower by the side of the road.

"I can see again. I can see again," he said over and over.

Read Luke 18:35-43

Lord, sometimes I cry out when I'm afraid or when things don't go right. It's hard to know you're there when things are bad. But, like Bartimaeus, I know you are there. Thank you, Jesus. Amen.

MEDITATION 20
NEVER TOO SHORT

I ran into the city of Jericho and headed for the market. I knew I would find other kids my age running around, looking for food or sometimes looking for trouble. I didn't have to go far for either in Jericho.

"Hey kid," I heard a voice calling from behind. "You on your way to Jerusalem?"

I turned to see a tall boy with a group of five or six other boys around him.

"Yeah," I said. "I'm following Jesus."

"Who's Jesus?" the boy asked.

"You mean you haven't heard about Jesus? Where have you been? *Everyone* knows who Jesus is. Even a blind beggar knew him."

I had insulted the boy, but I realized my mistake too late. He came closer and shoved me.

"Who cares about a blind beggar? I don't see Jesus now. All I see is this skinny kid in front of me who thinks he knows everything."

"I don't know everything. I just . . ."

But it was too late to explain. The boy pushed me down to the ground and started punching me. I protected myself as best I could. The boys around him laughed and shouted.

Just when I thought I couldn't stand it any longer, the punching stopped. I looked up between my hands to see the boy standing eye-to-eye with a bearded man who held him by the back of his coat.

"Got any taxes, little boy?" the man asked with a sneer.

The other boys laughed. I laughed too. I couldn't help it. The man's voice was squeaky. And what's more, the boy was an inch taller than the man.

The boy snapped back, "And just who are you to call me little? You're no bigger than my sister!"

It was an insult the boy shouldn't have spoken. Although he was small, the man was clearly stronger. He lifted the boy off the ground.

"My name is Zacchaeus. And I squeeze little people like you and your parents out of every cent they own. I'm the chief tax collector. Now, take your little friends and scram. Pick on someone your own size next time, like me!"

The other boys scattered as Zacchaeus roughly dropped the tall boy.

"Are you all right?" Zacchaeus asked.

"Yes, I think so," I said.

"There's no blood that I can see. You'll be fine. So tell me, what started all this? No, don't tell me. Let me guess. He called you the short end of a donkey. No, wait— he told you his sister could jump higher than you."

"No. None of that."

"So what was it?"

"I told him I was a follower of Jesus."

"Jesus? Who's Jesus?"

This time I didn't act surprised that someone didn't know Jesus.

"He's a rabbi. And he's the Messiah. He teaches people and heals them. He's going to Jerusalem. Some people say they're going to crown him king when he gets there."

Zacchaeus interrupted me by shaking his finger in my face.

"Now, don't lie, boy. I may be a cheater, but I don't like lying. Are you sure he's the Messiah? What else does he say?"

"He forgives people and tells them to repent, and . . ." I suddenly remembered Levi. "And he loves tax collectors too. One of his disciples used to be a tax collector."

Zacchaeus's face changed. "Where is this Jesus?" he asked.

"I don't know exactly where he is right now, but you could easily find him. He's surrounded by a big crowd."

We walked the streets until we came to the edge of a crowd that was moving along slowly. "He's probably in the middle of this crowd," I said.

Zacchaeus jumped up and down to see over the people.

"I can't see him. Can you get me closer? You said you were one of his disciples."

"Yes, but this crowd is huge. I'll never be able to get through."

Zacchaeus turned away sadly. As he did so I saw a tree in the distance.

"There!" I said. "Climb that tree! You can see him from there."

"You're right!" Zacchaeus's face brightened as we ran to the tree. "Can you see?" I called up to him when he settled onto a branch. He nodded and called back, "Yes, and he's coming this way!"

Jesus stopped right under the tree and looked up. "Zacchaeus, come down from the tree, won't you? I'd like to come to your house today."

Read Luke 19:1-10

Lord, you're worth climbing a tree for or getting beat up for! Thank you for loving me just the way I am. I don't have to worry about how I look or whether or not I'm strong. You made me special. Thanks a lot. Amen.

MEDITATION 21

JESUS PLANS AHEAD

After spending a day with Zacchaeus and his friends, we again headed toward Jerusalem. "Bartholomew and John, please go on ahead into Bethany," Jesus said. "As soon as you enter Bethany you'll see a small donkey that no one has ever ridden before. Untie it and bring it here."

"But won't that be stealing?" they asked.

"No. If the owner stops you, tell him the Lord needs it. He will understand."

I was puzzled by what Jesus said. I couldn't imagine just walking up to someone's animal and taking it. But Jesus' explanation was enough for Bartholomew and John, and they left for Bethany.

"Hey, wait for me!" I called out. If they were going to find a colt, I wanted a chance to ride it!

The three of us entered the village. Just as Jesus had told us, there was a small donkey tied to a tree.

"There it is!" I called out. "It's just like Jesus told us."

The donkey watched us approach. He backed away from me, but I held out my hand and spoke softly.

"It's OK, little fella. Jesus wants you. See? I won't hurt you." My soothing voice calmed him, and he stepped forward to smell my hand.

"He likes me," I said to the disciples behind me.

"Good. Let's untie him and take him back."

I started untying the leather strap when a voice called out.

"You there! What are you doing?"

I turned to see a gray-haired man carrying a bundle of sticks. The disciples tried to answer for me.

"Ah, well, it's like this. You see . . ."

I interrupted. "The Lord needs it. He sent us to get it for him," I said.

The man looked at me and the two disciples. "Well, why didn't you say so? Now this here's a good donkey. But mind you, he's never been ridden before. He might not take to strangers sitting on him. In fact, I was going to test him out with this bundle of sticks. But if the Lord needs him, why then go ahead, take him. Just return him when you're done."

I finished untying the straps. John thanked the man.

"Can I ride him?" I asked.

"No, Jesse. I don't think so," John said.

"Jesus must ride this colt first," Bartholomew added. "It's prophesied in the Holy Scriptures. Many years ago, a prophet named Zechariah predicted that the Messiah would come to Jerusalem riding a young donkey and that everyone would rejoice."

"So, Jesse, this donkey is just for the king, the Messiah," John concluded. "Do you understand?"

I nodded my head and spoke to the donkey.

"You'd better not drop him when he rides you."

The donkey's ears twitched at the sound of my voice.

"He's very special, you know. They say people will crown him king in Jerusalem. So you've got a special job. Don't let me down."

We soon joined Jesus and the other disciples.

"Thank you, friends," Jesus said. "Did you find the donkey as I said you would?"

"Yes. Just as you said," Bartholomew answered.

"Good. Remember, Jesse, everything I say will come to pass. Everything. Just believe and listen carefully."

"Yes, sir," I replied. The disciples put their coats onto the donkey.

"Jesus?" I asked him as he climbed onto the donkey.

"Yes, Jesse?"

"May I lead the colt for you?"

"Yes, my young friend, you may. I would be honored if you would serve me."

Read Luke 19:28-35

Lord, you planned ahead for a donkey to carry you. And you planned ahead to use me as a servant. Teach me to serve you well so that I might honor you and make you proud to call me your servant. I ask this in your name. Amen.

MEDITATION 22
KEEP LOOKING AHEAD

I took hold of the rope and led the donkey into the middle of the road.

"Jerusalem is straight ahead, Jesse. Keep your eyes on Jerusalem."

As soon as Jesus said this, the crowd began shouting and singing. "Blessed is the king who comes in the name of the Lord! Peace in heaven and glory in the highest!"

People grabbed palm branches as they walked and waved them in the air. The celebration went on for what seemed like miles.

What happened next was even more exciting. The crowd that walked ahead of us took off their coats and began to lay them on the road. I soon found myself walking on a carpet of coats!

All kinds of people laid down their coats. Some of the coats belonged to poor people. A few belonged to wealthy men and women. Many children laid down their small coats. And every once in a while we even walked on the coat of a Roman soldier. A Roman soldier could get into big trouble for being in a parade like this! I wondered if these people knew what they were doing.

I felt awkward walking on people's coats with my muddy sandals, so I reached down to take them off.

"Why are you taking off your sandals?" Jesus asked.

"It doesn't seem right," I said. "I'm stepping on all these coats, and I have mud on my sandals. I'm making the coats even more dirty."

"Why are you looking at the coats?" Jesus asked.

"Because I'm too embarrassed to look at the crowd. I don't belong in the middle of this parade, Jesus."

"You belong where you are," Jesus answered. "You are doing what I want you to do. Do not look at the coats, and do not look at the crowd, for the people who cheer you today will forget you tomorrow. They will not know your name or your face. They will not know what you did for me. That's why I told you to look straight ahead, Jesse. Look to Jerusalem. Serve me well and look ahead."

As Jesus spoke these words, I came to a place in the road where the layer of coats ended for a few feet. "There must be some people standing here who don't have coats," I thought. But as I looked to the side of the road, I saw who was standing there. These men indeed had coats. Long coats, in fact. The coats worn by the Pharisees.

"Jesus," the Pharisees cried out above the noise of the crowd, "make these people stop proclaiming you as king. And make them stop praising you."

Jesus laughed at them. "I tell you this, if I quiet the people, even the stones will cry out and praise me."

The Pharisees threw up their hands in anger. One shook his fist at Jesus. Another held his hands over his ears. Several more talked among themselves.

As we stepped off the coats and onto the road in front of the Pharisees, I realized I had not put my sandals back on.

"Ouch!" I cried out as I stepped on a sharp stone.

Jesus laughed again. "Sometimes," he said, "you'll get hurt when you do what I ask of you. And sometimes the stone-cold hearts of Pharisees will hurt you the most. Guard your heart against them, Jesse. They neither praise me nor do they love my servants. And put your sandals back on. There will be more stones ahead, I'm sure."

I smiled a little as I rubbed my sore foot. I had learned my lesson. My job was to lead his donkey and to keep my eyes straight ahead.

"On to Jerusalem, Jesse. We have work to do."

Read Luke 19:36-44

Lord, please help me to keep my eyes on you. Sometimes I see problems I can't begin to understand. And sometimes it's so much fun being a disciple of yours that it's easy to forget what you want me to do. Keep my eyes on the work that you ask me to do for you in this world. Amen.

MEDITATION 23
THIS IS GOD'S HOUSE

Although it was exciting to be with Jesus, it was difficult to understand what he did once he entered Jerusalem. He didn't stop to talk to people on the street. Instead, he headed straight to the temple. When he reached the temple courtyard, he began teaching.

One section of the courtyard was filled with tables. There people from all over the world brought their money and exchanged it for the money that was used inside the temple. Another section of the courtyard had fenced-in areas that were filled with animals. The loud noises of the animals took some getting used to.

"Why are there so many animals over there?" I asked Peter.

"Those animals are being sold to people who come from far away and don't have an animal with them to present to God. They exchange their money with the men over there, and buy the animals from these men over here."

Just then, Peter and I saw Jesus. He was standing in the middle of a group of sheep. His eyes burned with anger as he tore down the fences that held the animals. He drove them past the animal sellers with a stick. Then he threw over the tables and yelled at the money-changers to get out.

"You've turned this temple of prayer into a place for robbers. It's not right that you become rich on money from people who come to worship God. Now get out!"

The men were too afraid to argue. Hundreds of animals were running all around the courtyard. Some of them found the gate and escaped into the street.

I had never seen Jesus this angry, and the loud noises of the frightened animals scared me. In all the confusion, I ran out of the courtyard.

I heard Peter call as he ran after me. "Wait, Jesse!" he yelled. "Don't go out into the street. . . ." His voice trailed off as I ran into the center of the crowd.

What a mistake that was! The crowd soon turned into an angry mob. In the middle of all that yelling and shoving, all I could do was kneel down on the ground and cover my head. For a minute I thought I would be crushed.

But then I felt something soft rub against my arms. I opened my eyes slowly and looked up. Standing next to me was a very young lamb. She, too, was afraid of the crowd and had sought out the only other living thing his size—me.

"Hello there, little one," I said. I reached out to her and held her close to me. She bleated softly. Her body shook.

Suddenly, I was filled with new courage. "Out of the way!" I yelled at the people around me. I finally pushed my way to a nearby building.

The lamb and I watched the scene for several minutes. Soon the crowd calmed down, and people made their way back through the temple gates. When it seemed safe, the lamb and I followed closely behind. The courtyard was peaceful again. Most of the animals had been returned to their pens, and Jesus was teaching the crowd.

A group of Pharisees stood at the back of the crowd. They huddled in one corner of the courtyard and listened to Jesus. They mumbled to each other and made angry faces. I was curious, so I made my way over to listen.

"He's a messenger from Satan," one Pharisee said to another.

"I think he *is* Satan!" another one exclaimed.

"We've got to do something. The crowds think he's God!"

"I know. And *he* thinks he's God, too. He should be stoned for that!"

"Yes, but how do we do that? He's too popular with the people. They would end up stoning us."

"I don't know, but this can't go on. We've got to think of a plan."

"You're right. Jesus must die."

I couldn't believe my ears. We had come safely to Jerusalem only to face an enemy worse than robbers!

I stood there with my lamb as I watched the Pharisees continue their meeting. Cheers rose from the crowd with each new teaching from Jesus.

Right then I knew that my life with Jesus would never be the same.

Read Luke 19:45-46

Lord, I'm sorry if I sometimes forget that the church is a special place for you. Teach me to respect the building and the people who serve there. In your name, Amen.

MEDITATION 24

THE BIGGEST GIFT OF ALL

Our time in Jerusalem was filled with both excitement and fear. We left our campsite on the Mount of Olives each morning and entered the city. Every day I brought my lamb with me on a rope.

Jesus taught in the temple. One afternoon Jesus spent quite a bit of time talking with Pharisees and teachers. They were trying to get him to say bad things about God, the Scriptures, or the Romans by asking him questions. None of their tricks worked, however. Jesus embarrassed the Pharisees with his answers. The crowds thought it was great fun.

At the end of one his talks, Jesus walked toward another part of the temple area and asked us to join him.

"Look, men," he said. He pointed to the offering boxes. The money from the offering was used to keep the temple looking nice and to pay the people who worked there.

"Do you see the rich men? They give quite a bit, don't they?"

"I'll say," said Judas. "Why, that one gave what most people earn in a year."

"Yes, indeed," Jesus said.

The disciples thought Jesus was pleased. It certainly was a lot of money.

"But look," Jesus said. "Watch this next woman."

An older woman whose husband had died came to the offering box. She took two copper coins from her bag and placed them in the box.

"Now that's what I call cheap!" Judas said.

Jesus did not look at Judas. He looked at the woman. "Not so, my disciple. It may appear that the woman gave less than the others. But she actually put in much more than all the others combined. The others were rich and gave part of what they had. They still have plenty left over. But that woman gave everything she had left. She has no money left now because she loves God so much."

"Judas," Jesus continued, "you're too good at counting money. Be sure you also count what is in people's hearts."

Judas grumbled a bit. The disciples and Jesus walked back to the crowd. I stayed behind.

I couldn't help watching the poor woman as she shuffled away from the offering box. "If she has no money, how will she pay for the things she needs?" I thought to myself. I remembered the days when I was a beggar and had no one to live with or to look after me. My lamb tugged at the end of the rope impatiently. And that gave me a great idea.

"I'll catch up with you in a second," I said to Peter, who was waiting for me.

"Ma'am!" I called out as I ran. She did not stop until I caught up with her and pulled on her sleeve.

"Excuse me," I said again. "I'd like to give you this."

I gave her the rope that held my lamb. The lamb was complaining loudly about being made to run so quickly.

"But why?" the woman asked. She sounded confused.

"Because of Jesus," I said. "I'm one of his disciples. This lamb and I have become friends, but you need him more than I do. Take him."

The woman looked at me and smiled. "God bless you, my child. God bless you," she said as she walked away.

"Goodbye," I said as I turned to run to Jesus. My joy grew with each step. I jumped into his arms, and he held me close.

I shed a few tears that day, but they were happy tears. I was sad that wouldn't see my little lamb anymore, but I was happy for the woman who had found help that day. Now I knew why that little lamb had followed me—just for that reason.

Read Luke 21:1-4

Lord, help me to give whatever I can to you. It's easy to hold on to money, but you want me to be generous. Teach me to give as if my gift were the most important thing to you and the least important thing to me.

MEDITATION 25

NOT EVERYONE LOVED JESUS

Jerusalem was a wonderful city to explore. It was filled with people from all over the world. And the marketplace was the biggest I had ever seen.

On one of my late afternoon walks through the city, I noticed Judas out walking too. He was just a few blocks ahead of me, so I ran to catch up to him.

But as I got closer, something in the way Judas was walking told me that his mission was not a good one. His shoulders were hunched over, and he stuck close to the buildings. Every now and then he looked over his shoulder. I decided to follow him secretly.

Judas turned down a dark side street and stopped in front of a building. I hid in the doorway of the building next door. Judas knocked, and I heard the creak of a door and quiet voices.

I couldn't follow Judas into the building, so I climbed the steps to the roof. Below me was the shadowy courtyard where Judas stood speaking to some men.

"Are you sure you want to do this for us?" a man asked Judas.

"Yes."

"Remember, this was your idea. Don't accuse us later of forcing you into this," another man told him.

"No, I won't," Judas answered. "I've had enough of Jesus. I'll be happy to turn him over to you."

My heart stopped cold. My head spun. I thought I was going to be sick. I couldn't believe what I had just heard! I wanted to cry out, but I kept silent. Judas continued.

"You know," he said, "doing this won't be easy—it could be risky for me. If Peter ever got wind of this, he'd kill me. I think I ought to be paid for my work."

"So it's not just for the cause of Israel that you do this, eh?" a Pharisee asked.

"Let's just say I want *everyone* to be happy over Jesus' death. A little silver wouldn't hurt. And certainly you gentlemen have enough silver."

"Very well. How much then?"

"50 pieces will do."

"No. Too much. We could hire an archer to have him killed for less than that. We'll give you ten pieces."

"You insult me," Judas said. "An archer can miss. Thirty pieces or tomorrow I'll go back to the crowds and tell them about your plan. You'll have thousands of people tearing down these walls to take you out and stone you."

The men looked at each other. The oldest one nodded quietly.

"Agreed," the leader said. "But you must understand that we can't capture Jesus when there's a crowd around. That means you'll need to lead us to his camp in the dark."

Before the men finished speaking, I climbed down the steps to the street. Once safely there, I ran back through the darkening streets to the temple. Jesus and the rest of the disciples had gone back to camp. The sun had just set, and all that remained of the day was a red glow in the west and a few stars in the sky. I looked up to the Mount of Olives. I knew Jesus had to be there somewhere.

"Oh no! He's gone back already!" I said out loud. I ran through the city gate, but it was dark by the time I found the road to our camp. I tried to locate our campsite on the hillside, but I couldn't pick out the spot. I couldn't see the trees or boulders that would show me the way, either.

"Jesus!" I yelled. "Where are you?"

There was no reply.

"Jesus!" I yelled again.

I knew it was useless to climb—it was way too dark. I sat down beside a tall tree and cried softly. I prayed, "Dear Father, I'm lost. I need to find Jesus so that I can warn him about Judas. Please help me. Amen." Within minutes, my tired body and the strain of the day caught up with me. I fell sound asleep.

Read Luke 22:1-6

Lord, it's hard to imagine that I would ever not love you. Keep me from forgetting that you are God and that you love me so much. Teach me to be loyal to you. Amen.

MEDITATION 26
A MEAL TO REMEMBER

Jesus found me the next morning.
"Let's go, Jesse," he said as he shook me awake.
"Jesus!" I said. "I have to tell you about Judas . . ."
Jesus stopped me. "I know already. You don't need to tell me. Right now we must find the others so that we can celebrate the Passover together."

I quietly followed Jesus as he explained everything that would happen to him. Then he said, "Don't worry, Jesse. Everything will go as God directs."

It wasn't until we arrived in Jerusalem and heard Andrew's cheery voice that I smiled.

"Right this way, gentlemen," Andrew announced as if he were a waiter. "Dinner is served." Everyone laughed. Everyone, that is, except Peter. He was staring at me. His eyes were angry and his nose flared.

"And just where were *you*, young man? I told you to . . ."
Jesus raised his hand. "It's OK, Peter. He got lost last night. He was frightened and slept at the foot of the hill. Come, let's celebrate! It's Passover. No scolding allowed until Passover is over. Don't you remember? The eldest child was saved on the Passover."

John chuckled and Levi laughed openly at Peter.
"He's right, old man," Levi said. "Save your anger for some other prank the boy might get into. Let's eat. I'm starved."

There was no servant in the room to wash our feet. To our surprise, Jesus himself took a towel and some water, knelt down, and washed our feet!

When he was done, Jesus led everyone in a song before our meal. Then he took some bread and said, "This is my body. Eat this bread as a way of remembering my body." He broke the bread into pieces and gave it to the disciples.

After supper he took the wine and gave some to the disciples. "This wine is to remind you of the new promise I make in my blood," Jesus said.

It was hard for the disciples to accept Jesus' words. We still did not want him to die. And yet we could see in his eyes that what he said was true. John was sad and laid his head on Jesus. Several of the disciples cried.

Then Jesus said something that made my heart skip.

"The man who dips into the dish with me will betray me."

I looked quickly at Jesus and Judas. Both were dipping their bread into the dish—no one else was! I thought that at any moment the other disciples would jump off their couches and tackle Judas!

But to my surprise, no one did anything. Rather than looking at the table for someone's hand, the disciples questioned each other. To make matters worse, they started arguing again about who would be the greatest in Jesus' kingdom.

Jesus interrupted. "Stop arguing, all of you! Don't you remember my teaching? The one who serves will be the greatest in the kingdom. Did you see how I served you when we came into the room by washing your feet? Do the same to one another and you will be great. You will also be great if you suffer the way I will suffer. It will be difficult, but you will follow me. Peter, you will have the hardest time."

"Me?" Peter asked. He looked surprised.

"Yes. I've been praying for you. Before the rooster crows, you will deny me. But you will come back. And then you'll encourage and take care of the others."

"But Lord, I'm ready to go to prison for you. I'm ready to die for you! How can you say I will deny you?" Peter looked hurt and angry.

"Peter, before the rooster crows tomorrow morning you will deny three times that you know me."

The disciples were shocked that Peter would do such a thing. I was shocked too. I didn't think Peter would ever leave Jesus. I wondered if God had changed his mind—maybe Judas would not betray Jesus. I was lost in my thoughts until Jesus spoke.

"Men," Jesus said, "it's time to go. Follow me."

Read Luke 22:14-20

Lord, I forget things a lot. I forget homework. I forget to clean my room. I forget to send thank-you letters. But teach me never to forget that you died for me on purpose. You died to save me from my sin.

MEDITATION 27

STAY AWAKE!

"You wouldn't really say you didn't know Jesus, would you?" I asked Peter as we walked back to the Mount of Olives. Jesus had asked us to join him for prayer in a garden there.

"No, Jesse. I wouldn't. Not ever. Sometimes Jesus uses words differently. He must mean something different than what it sounds like to us."

"Yeah, maybe," I said. Peter had become special to me. He was like my father now, and I was as hurt as he was by what Jesus said about him. "I'll stand by you no matter what happens," I said to Peter.

"Thanks, kid. I know you will."

We arrived at the garden in the dark and found a nice open space where we could sit and pray. Andrew set about making a fire.

"I'm going to pray alone," Jesus said. "I want all of you to stay here and pray. Pray that you won't be tempted to give up your faith." Jesus walked a short distance away.

"Why does he keep talking that way? Who does he think we are?" The disciples discussed among themselves. "We have followed him for three years. We gave up our businesses. We gave up our homes. Now he thinks we're going to leave him!"

"I know why," I said out loud. "Jesus said that we should pray because one of us has already betrayed him."

"What do you mean? I haven't done anything!" Peter exclaimed.

"I'm talking about Judas. He dipped into the dish when Jesus spoke," I told Peter.

"That's nonsense," Thomas said. "Judas is a good guy. He may be a little cranky sometimes, but he's no traitor. You've got an active imagination."

"But I'm not imagining, Thomas! If Judas is one of us, why isn't he here?" Judas was nowhere in sight.

"I thought he walked up with you, Bartholomew," John said.

"No. I thought he was up front with Peter."

The disciples began discussing where Judas might be. Peter interrupted. "Listen, Jesus asked us to pray, so let's pray."

Everyone agreed and talked briefly about Jesus' death. Many of us cried. All of us prayed.

"Father in heaven," I began. "Please don't let Jesus die. He hasn't done anything wrong. Stop the men who want to kill him. And help me to be a good disciple. Help me to stand by Jesus no matter what happens. Please, God. Please!" I prayed for several more minutes and then opened my eyes to see if anyone else was finished.

They were more than finished. They were sleeping. They had been sad about what Jesus told them—so sad that they had become very tired. They had also bundled up against the cold night air. Within minutes after they started to pray, the disciples had fallen asleep.

I was tempted to wake them, but I decided to join Jesus instead. I found him kneeling by a nearby rock. He looked up to heaven and prayed.

"Please, Father, if you're willing, don't let me die on the cross." He paused as if waiting for an answer. "But if that's what you want, I'll do it." Jesus bowed his head and clenched his hands. His whole body shook and he began sweating heavily.

As I stepped closer to Jesus, I stepped on a twig, and a loud crack broke the silence.

"Jesse?" Jesus asked. "Is that you?"

"Yes, Jesus," I answered.

"Did you pray?"

"Yes, I did."

"And the others. Are they praying?"

"They prayed, but they're asleep now."

Jesus hung his head down. He looked sad and frustrated. "Let's go. We'll wake them up. They must pray!"

We walked back to the campfire.

"Wake up!" Jesus called out. "You must pray before the battle!"

James began to explain why they had slept, but it was too late. We heard the sound of voices on the hillside below us and saw the glow of torches.

The time had come.

Read Luke 22:39-46

Lord, I know how the disciples felt, I think. I sometimes want to do anything other than pray. Help me to remember to pray and to pray often. It's important to you. Help it to be as important to me. Amen.

MEDITATION 28
LET GOD DO THE FIGHTING

"Jesse! Get behind the rocks there, quickly!"

I obeyed Jesus immediately. The noise of the crowd and the glow of torches came closer. Jesus knew that this was no place for a kid. I peered from between the rocks as the crowd arrived.

Peter and the others stood next to Jesus as the crowd stopped. No one moved except the leader of the crowd—Judas. This was the night he had chosen to betray Jesus.

"I was right after all!" I thought.

Judas held Jesus and kissed him on the cheek.

"Judas, are you betraying me with a kiss?" Jesus asked.

Judas stood back. He knew that a kiss was meant to show love. It was the way friends greeted one another in our country. Judas was no friend of Jesus.

I couldn't wait behind the rock any longer. My Master was about to be taken and killed by the crowd. But what could I do? My eyes glanced over by our fire and locked onto shining metal. Swords! We had two swords!

I realized the swords would be of no use if they laid on the ground out of reach of the disciples. I slowly crept along the ground to see if I could get the swords. The crowd and the disciples had started to argue. No one paid attention to me.

Seeing my chance, I rushed to the swords. I picked them up and ran up behind Andrew, who stood in the back.

"Andrew," I whispered, pulling on his arm.

He spun around nervously.

"You frightened me to death! What do you want?" he whispered.

"I've got the swords from the campsite. Pass one up to Peter," I said.

Andrew grabbed both swords. "Peter!" he called out. "Here!"

Andrew threw one of the swords through the air. Peter caught it by the handle and in the same motion swung it up with a yell: "I told you I would die for you!"

The blade glistened in the light of the torches as it came down. A priest jumped out of the way, but in doing so he pushed his servant into the path of the sword. The blade sliced through the servant's ear.

"Enough!" Jesus ordered, holding up his arm. Peter was about to take another swing but stopped at the sound of Jesus' command. The men in the crowd also stopped their attempt at fighting back. They stood silently, watching Jesus. He called the man forward who was holding his head in pain.

Jesus took the man's hand away from his head and touched his ear. The bleeding stopped and his ear was healed.

"Am I a leader of some rebellion against Israel? Is that what you think I've been doing these last three years with fishermen, tax collectors, and sinners? Is that why you've come out here with swords and clubs to arrest me?" Jesus questioned the crowd.

The crowd was silent.

"I spent weeks in the middle of the temple courtyard where you could have arrested me. But here you are, doing your work in the dark. That is no surprise. You do things in the dark because you are afraid and ashamed to do them when it is day."

The elders and high priests were angry at what Jesus said. They rushed forward and grabbed his arms. They led him away from the middle of the disciples.

Jesus looked over his shoulder at us as he was led gruffly away. "The time has begun," he said. "Remember to pray."

We watched as the temple guards tied his hands and led him down the hill toward the city. Peter dropped his sword. John fell to the ground and began to cry.

Read Luke 22:47-53

Lord, I wish I could solve all my problems my way. Kids at school can make fun of me or other kids. That makes me really mad. Teach me to not be angry. Teach me a better way to solve problems—your way. Amen.

MEDITATION 29
HURTING A GOOD FRIEND

"I'm going to follow them," Peter said. "I said I would stand by him. I'm not going back on my word." The crowd leading Jesus away was several hundred yards down the path.

"But they'll capture you, too," John argued. "They've already seen you cut off a man's ear. And you almost killed a priest!"

"I don't care. I've got to stay with Jesus."

The other disciples began talking loudly, trying to convince Peter that he shouldn't go. It did no good. Peter picked up his coat and headed down the mountain. The others stood watching.

"Peter, wait!" I yelled. "I'm coming with you."

"No!" Peter spun around and pointed at me. I stood dead in my tracks. "Not this time! You can't come this time. This is not a party. This is not a boat trip. This is not an adventure. You will stay here with the others."

I had never seen Peter so angry. "John, take care of the boy and don't let him out of your sight. We'll meet somewhere on the mountain when this is all over. Better yet, let's meet tomorrow in the temple courtyard."

John took me by the shoulder and led me to the campfire. The others stood, not knowing what to do or say.

"John, what are you going to do?" I asked.

Suddenly John remembered Jesus' words. "We have to pray now, my friends. We didn't stay awake before when Jesus asked us. Let's not fail him again."

We knelt around the campfire and prayed. James began, then Andrew prayed, and then John. Each one prayed and prayed. Some cried softly for Jesus. Others whispered prayers as another prayed out loud.

We had prayed for about half an hour when I became restless. "I wish I could follow Peter," I thought. I looked around and spotted a torch that the servant of the priest had dropped. It was within my reach, so I picked up the torch and lit it in the fire. Quietly, I stood up and tiptoed past the disciples. No one stirred—they were all deep in prayer.

I ran as swiftly as I could down the hillside toward Jerusalem. Peter's words came back to me, "I'm ready to die for you, Lord!" I was afraid that Peter would try something foolish.

I arrived at the temple courtyard where I met a guard.

"Do you know where they took Jesus?" I asked.

"Who wants to know?" the guard asked.

I realized my answer could get me in trouble. I had to think fast.

"I'm carrying one of the priest's torches. He left it on the Mount of Olives."

"Well, in that case," the guard said, "they're at the chief elder's house. It's two blocks north."

"Thank you, sir," I said as I ran out of the temple gate.

When I arrived at the chief elder's house, the door of the courtyard was open. Jesus sat at the far end of the house with the elders and priests. Peter was in a corner of the courtyard warming himself by the fire. I wondered how he'd gotten in without being noticed. "Perhaps the crowd that arrested Jesus isn't here," I thought.

I put out my torch and entered the courtyard quietly. I hid in the opposite corner so that Peter would not see me. Several other people sat with Peter around the fire.

"You there," I heard one woman say to Peter. "You're a disciple of Jesus, aren't you?"

"You must be mistaken. I don't even know the man," Peter answered.

"Oh, but you must be," another said.

"No, I'm not!" Peter argued a second time.

"Jesus is in for big trouble," another man around the fire said. He stopped and looked up at Peter. "And you are one his followers. Don't deny it! You even talk like one of them."

Peter's face glared with anger.

"I don't know what you're talking about!" he yelled. "I am not a follower of Jesus Christ!"

Peter's words echoed in the courtyard.

I felt my heart sink. Jesus looked across the courtyard at Peter without anger or sadness.

And then the rooster crowed.

Peter sobbed as he ran out into the street.

Read Luke 22:54-62

Lord, please keep me close to you so that I don't ever hurt you. When someone asks if I'm a Christian, let me say "Yes!" In your name, Amen.

MEDITATION 30

TURN THE OTHER CHEEK

I thought I might try to follow Peter to see if I could comfort him, but he ran off too quickly. So I stayed in the courtyard to hear more about what the men might do to Jesus.

"We've heard enough!" said one of the men talking with Jesus. "Let's get a couple of hours of sleep before we take him before the full council."

"You're right," another agreed.

"Guards!" the first man called out. "Stay with this criminal until morning. And station a guard at the entrance to the courtyard. We don't want any more of his followers hanging around here. If you see any, arrest them."

I shrunk back behind the bush, praying that no one would see me.

I could see Jesus through the branches, though. And what I saw angered and frightened me. After the elders and priests left, the guards blindfolded Jesus and pushed him to his knees. Then they began to beat him. What's worse, they made a game out of it.

"Who just hit you?" one guard said as he hit Jesus in the face. "Come on, prophet. You're supposed to know everything. Who hit you?"

Another man kicked Jesus in the back, laughing as he did so.

As I watched, I remembered the words that Jesus had spoken three years earlier on the mountain. He had said that if someone strikes you on one cheek, you should turn and offer him the other cheek also. I knew that Jesus had the power to break free from his ropes and stop the guards. He simply chose not to.

My anger turned to tears. I couldn't watch any longer. I held my hands over my ears to keep from hearing the soldiers strike Jesus' body. Most of all, I couldn't stand to hear the guards insult my Master. It seemed like the night would never end.

When the sky got brighter toward dawn, Jesus was still kneeling. He was still bound tightly, and his head was bowed as if praying. The guards had grown tired of their game and had left Jesus alone. They sat by a fire a short way from Jesus. A few of them slept.

I looked closely to be sure the guards weren't watching. Then, very quietly, I tiptoed behind the bushes that surrounded the courtyard. I kneeled behind Jesus.

"Jesus," I whispered.

He opened his eyes and looked up. His face was swollen and bleeding. He did not speak.

"Here," I said. "Take some water."

I reached out and gave him a drink of water from the waterskin I carried. He sipped the water slowly.

"Are you all right?" I asked.

He nodded. "You can't stay here, Jesse," he finally whispered. "Go and find the other disciples. Stay with them."

I nodded. I did not know whether or not I could find them, but I would try.

"Do you want them to come and help you?" I asked.

"No!" Jesus spoke louder, coughing. "No. My time has come. Don't stop what needs to be done. Only my Father can stop it."

"But . . ."

"Don't argue. And Jesse?"

"Yes."

"What did you learn tonight?"

"That it's hard to be a disciple. Sometimes it makes you cry."

"Good boy, Jesse. You've learned well. Now go. The guards will take me away soon."

"Yes sir."

I reached out and touched Jesus' hair. He pressed his head against my hand and closed his eyes.

"Goodbye, Jesse. I will see you again."

Read Luke 22:63-65

Lord, teach me to keep silent if other kids make fun of me. It doesn't do any good to fight back with words. You know how it hurts to have others make fun of you, so please help me do what you did. Amen.

MEDITATION 31

JESUS IS THE SON OF GOD

After talking with Jesus I went back to my hiding place. Soon several priests marched through the gate and into the courtyard.

"Get up, you lazy dogs!" one of the priests yelled to the guards. "You were supposed to guard the criminal, not have a party with him. Grab him and follow us to the temple. We've got to take him before the council of elders."

The guards who had been sleeping rubbed their eyes and got up slowly. The other guards had already lifted Jesus off his knees.

I hid closer to the ground. I could easily be seen in the daylight if I wasn't careful.

The guards led Jesus out into the street behind the priests. Moments later, I came out of my hiding place and went to the gate. I looked up the street and saw that Jesus and the others were a safe distance away from me. I followed them, acting like any other boy in Jerusalem out on an early morning errand.

The group made its way to the temple. It was early enough so that no crowds would be there to stop the priests from treating Jesus badly. The Pharisees and elders had planned Jesus' capture well. They captured him during the night, and now they would put him on trial early in the morning. There were no witnesses around to complain or to start a riot.

I entered the courtyard of the temple without being noticed and followed Jesus. They took him to a large room where the entire council was waiting. I passed by the door quickly, and saw that the council was made up of Pharisees and teachers and priests. I quickly crossed the hall and hid around a corner. I could still see Jesus through the doorway.

Several of the men on the council felt bad and complained loudly to the council about how the guards had treated Jesus.

"What does it matter?" the chief priest said. "He's guilty anyway. Let's get on with this trial."

The council asked him questions.

"Are you the Messiah we've been waiting for?" a teacher asked.

"You won't believe my answer so I won't tell you. All you need to know is that I will be seated in heaven at the right hand of God the Father," answered Jesus.

"Are you saying that you are the Son of God?" a Pharisee shouted in anger.

Jesus stared at the man who asked.

"You are correct in saying that."

The room was silent for just a second as everyone gasped. Loud arguments soon began. One man's voice bellowed above everyone else's.

"You heard what he just said. We don't need any more information. He has cursed God by saying that he is the Son of God!"

Many others shouted in agreement. "This man must die!"

"Moses told us to kill anyone who claimed such a thing."

"Death! Death!" several chanted.

Only a few shook their heads. "No! Listen to him! Let him explain," they cried. But it was no use.

"Order, order!" the chief priest shouted as he banged on the table. It took several minutes for the room to become quiet.

"It is true," said the chief priest. "This man has spoken a sinful thing. And it is true he must die. But the Romans will not allow us to kill anyone unless they find that person guilty of one of their crimes. They don't care about our God. We're helpless to do anything about punishing this man."

"Take him to Pilate," a Pharisee called out. "Let the Romans kill him."

Many in the council shouted in agreement.

"So be it," the chief priest said. "Guards, take this man and follow us to Pilate." He turned to another priest and ordered, "Run ahead of us to Pilate and request a meeting on our behalf. Tell him it is urgent. Tell him that we caught a rebel who needs to be tried."

"But if Pilate asks what the man has done, what should I tell him?"

"Tell him that this Jesus opposes paying taxes to Caesar and that he says he is king. That will get Pilate's attention."

I watched the chief priest and the others leave the room. The guards pushed Jesus along. The situation didn't look hopeful for Jesus.

"Perhaps this Pilate can help us," I thought. "He has no reason to hate Jesus like these elders do." My hope was renewed, and I worked on a plan. I still hoped that God would allow Jesus to live.

"Maybe Pilate can stop the council," I thought. "And maybe I can help."

Read Luke 22:66-71

Lord, saying what's right isn't always popular. You told the people you were God. They didn't like that. Help me when I tell kids that you are God. Give me courage. Amen.

MEDITATION 32

HE IS INNOCENT!

I left the courtyard before the chief priest's messenger. I hoped to somehow reach Pilate before him. "Perhaps I could convince this Pilate that Jesus is innocent," I thought. "But how? He probably wouldn't even listen to a thirteen-year-old boy."

Lost in my thoughts, I raced around a corner and ran straight into a horse. It reared back, and its rider almost fell to the ground.

I looked up to see a Roman soldier in the saddle.

"I'm sorry, sir. I didn't mean to scare your horse."

The soldier laughed. "That's all right, son. Just watch where you're going." He clicked his heels against the horse and made his way down the street.

When the soldier was just a few yards away, I realized that I had seen him once before. It was Artemis's master! He was the Centurion who had asked Jesus to heal Artemis. Jesus had told us that this man's faith was greater than any other in Israel. "But what is he doing in Jerusalem?" I wondered as I watched his horse trot away.

"Wait, wait!" I called out after him. "Sir, please wait!"

The horse stopped, and the Roman soldier turned around.

"Yes, son?"

"Do you remember me?"

"Can't say that I do."

"A couple of years ago you came to Jesus and asked him to heal your servant Artemis."

"That's right! How did you know?"

"I was there. I am a follower of Jesus."

"Ah, so you're Artemis's little friend. He talks about you once in a while. He always wondered what became of the boy who used to eat my leftover suppers."

"Yes, that was me," I said.

"And now you're in Jerusalem because Jesus is here, right?"

I nodded.

"It's wonderful, isn't it? Even thought I'm a Roman soldier, I think it would be wonderful to have Jesus as king instead of Herod or Caesar. Don't you?"

"Then you haven't heard!" I exclaimed.

"Heard what?"

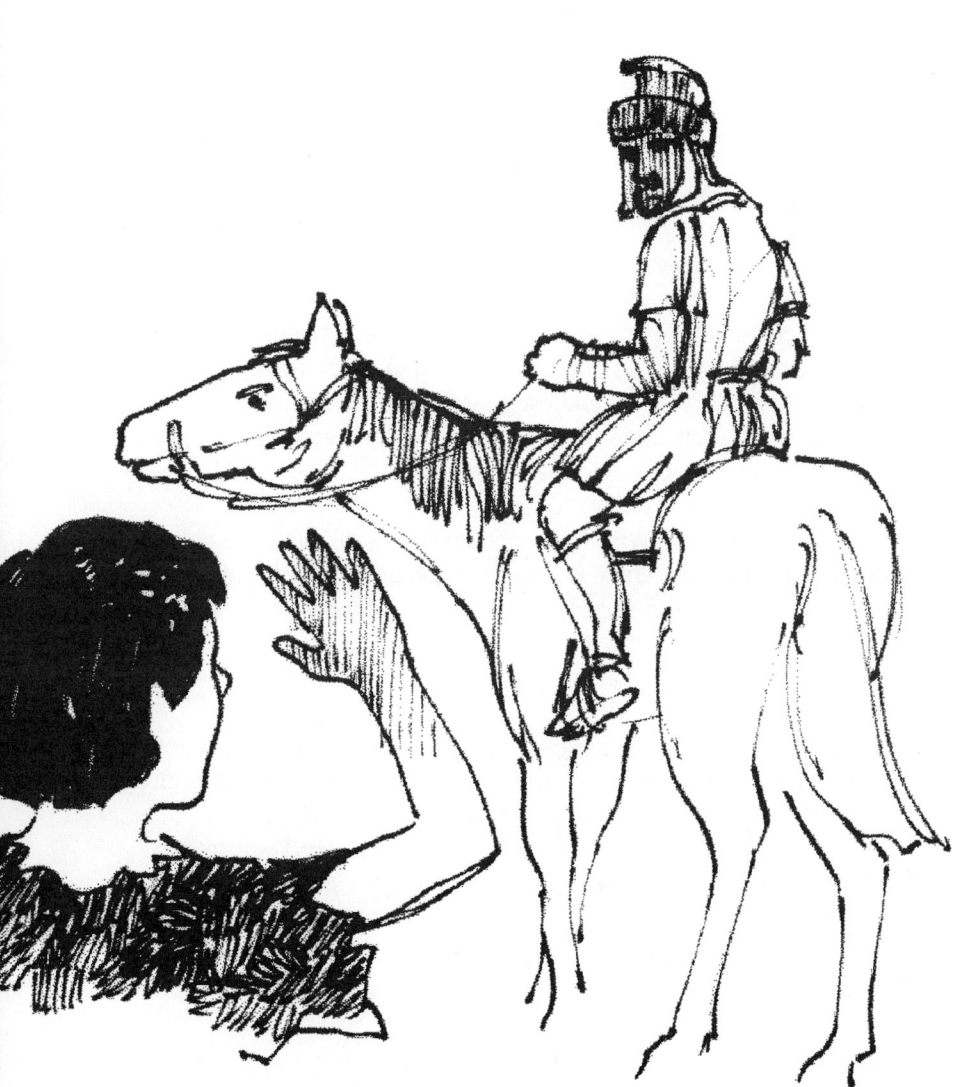

"Jesus has been arrested. The chief priests and elders have put him on trial and want him killed. They're going to Pilate right now. They're accusing him of leading a rebellion and telling people they shouldn't pay taxes. Can you help?"

"I'd like to, but how?"

"You can go to Pilate. Tell him these things aren't true. Tell him what Jesus did for Artemis. Tell him all the things Jesus did for other people. Tell him, please!"

"I'm on my way. Pilate will be certain to listen to reason."

"Can I come?"

The officer hesitated for a moment.

"All right, come on. Climb on board."

He grabbed me by the arm and pulled me up onto his saddle. I held my arms around his waist, and we took off. Within moments we stopped in front of Pilate's house.

"Quickly," I said. "There's a messenger on his way from the chief priests. I'm sure we got here before him, but we have no time to lose!"

We dismounted and marched into Pilate's house. The guards on the street did not stop us because my new friend was a Roman officer.

"I'm here to see Pilate," he told the guard inside the courtyard.

The guard led us up some winding stairs. He announced our presence to Pilate, who sat behind a table reading papers.

"What is it?" he asked impatiently.

"My name is Anthony. I'm a Centurion from Galilee. I've come on a matter of great urgency. There is a man named Jesus whom the Jews will be bringing to you for trial."

"On what grounds?" Pilate asked.

"That he opposes paying taxes and that he claims to be king of the Jews."

"King? Foolishness. That's not a problem. There are lunatics all over this city claiming to be king of the Jews. Even Herod thinks he's a king. Hah, what a joke! But this business about the taxes, is it true?"

Anthony looked to me for the answer. I told Pilate how Jesus had taught people that they should pay to Caesar whatever belonged to Caesar, and that they should pay to God whatever belonged to God.

"I see," Pilate rubbed his chin. "I appreciate your coming, Anthony. These Jews are a nuisance. They're always arguing about something. Honestly, I wish I were back in Rome instead of stuck in this dump called Jerusalem."

Anthony chuckled a little. "Whatever you can do to help us would be appreciated, Pilate. I'm sure you'll be wise in your decision."

Pilate motioned for us to leave. "Of course, of course. Now run along. I've got work to do."

Read Luke 23:1-3

Lord, teach me to trust only you. Some people may seem like they can help me and solve my problems. But they're just people too. And some people like Pilate don't always do what God wants. Teach me to depend on you for everything. Amen.

MEDITATION 33
HE IS GUILTY

Anthony was sure that Pilate would let Jesus go.

I smiled a little, but my heart sank when I saw the messenger from the temple. He had just pushed past the guard and was on his way up the stairs to meet Pilate. We saw the chief priests leading Jesus toward us as we entered the street below.

"See?" I said to Anthony. "They've beaten him. And now they're bringing him here."

Anthony and I waited outside in the doorway of the building across the street. A large crowd was gathering below Pilate's balcony. They all talked about Jesus.

"He's a rebel, I tell you," one of the temple guards said out loud. "I hear the Romans were about to send another legion of soldiers here to make us suffer for Jesus' crimes!"

Anthony knew the guard was telling a lie in order make the crowd angry. It worked. The crowd turned into a mob that shouted and shook their fists in the air.

"That's not all—he also claimed to be God," the guard continued. "He said so this morning right in front of the elders. You know what that means!"

"I say he's not a man at all," another man joined him. "I say he's Satan, and we ought to kill him right now!"

No one in the crowd stood up for Jesus. Pilate was Jesus' only hope now, as far as I could see.

We stood there for what seemed like hours. A rumor began in the crowd that Pilate had sent Jesus to Herod through another door. "Stay here," someone said. "Herod's a chicken and won't try him. He'll send him back to Pilate, no doubt!"

It was the middle of the morning when Pilate and Jesus stepped onto the balcony overlooking the crowds. Some of the elders stood behind Pilate.

"Listen, people," Pilate began. "This man hasn't done anything wrong. But I'll give you a choice. I can either set this Jesus free or I can free the killer Barabbas. Whom would you prefer to have on the streets with you?"

My heart leaped and pounded with joy. "Thank you, God. I knew you would change your mind!" I clung to Anthony with excitement.

But my joy did not last long.

"Kill him! Kill him!" Voices yelled out from the mob and from the elders on the balcony.

Others cried out, "Let Barabbas go!"

"Who's Barabbas?" I asked.

"The worst criminal I've ever seen," Anthony answered. "He's the reason I came to Jerusalem. I captured him in Galilee on charges of killing someone. He had started riots in my area. He then escaped, and I followed him here and had him thrown in prison."

Anthony could not stay silent any longer. "No! He is innocent!" he shouted. "Let him go. Barabbas is a murderer!" He tried hard, but no one listened. They were too busy yelling at Pilate.

Pilate threw up his hands and walked back inside with Jesus and the priests. Within moments, Jesus and the priests were in the street. Eight Roman guards surrounded Jesus as they walked through the crowd. The crowd pushed and shoved. They yelled curses at Jesus and shook their fists. Some people spat at him.

"What will they do, Anthony?" I asked. "Will they let him go?"

"I'm afraid not, Jesse. They're going to crucify him. It's over, Jesse. It's too late."

Read Luke 23:13-25

Lord, there are some days when life just doesn't seem fair. I know that you control everything that happens in this world. Teach me to not get upset when things don't go the way I would like them to. Amen.

MEDITATION 34

A HELPER FROM AFRICA

Jesus was led down the street as the crowds jeered all around him. From time to time I could see Jesus through the crowd as he tried to stay standing. He was so tired that he stumbled several times.

I couldn't watch any longer. I jumped into the crowd and began pushing and yelling, "Out of my way!"

Anthony tried to stop me, but it was too late. I got lost in the crowd and moved along with it as if it were a river. My shouts and pushing helped me move through the flood of people toward the front of the line. "You shouldn't be so eager to see a crucifixion, boy," one man yelled at me as I pushed by. "Your stomach might not be ready for it," he laughed.

By the time I made my way to the front of the crowd, Jesus was outside the city walls. In the distance I saw the place they called Golgotha. That's where they were taking Jesus.

"Carry your crossbeam!" I heard a soldier command Jesus.

Jesus reached out his arms to hold the beam but it slipped from his hands. It was too heavy for him now that he was so weak.

"I said carry it!" the soldier shouted at him. This time he added the sting of a whip to his command. It didn't do any good. Jesus fell to his knees.

"Jesus!" I cried. I pushed forward to help, but I was stopped by another soldier before I was able to reach him.

"Get out of here, runt! This is no game. Go home!" The Roman solider pushed me aside. I fell against a man standing by his camel.

"Whoa, son! You're getting yourself into trouble, I see. This doesn't look like a place for a lad. You're in the way of these Roman soldiers today. They're out to have their sport by killing another innocent victim."

I looked up at the man. His clothes and his dark face told me he was not from Israel.

"Are you making fun of us?" a Roman guard asked from behind me. He looked angrily at the stranger.

"Certainly not," the stranger said. "I was merely pointing out to the boy here that you Romans seem fond of accusing innocent men." Several people in the crowd laughed.

"And where are you from?" the soldier asked.

"From Cyrene, my dear sir. My name is Simon. I'm a merchant by trade, in the business of trading fine African goods." He bowed and smiled, unafraid of the soldier.

"A wise guy, are you? Well, welcome to Jerusalem, Simon of Cyrene." The soldier pretended to be pleasant but soon turned nasty. "Your first job here will be to carry this man's crossbeam. Let's go! Now! Before I throw you in prison."

The soldier grabbed Simon.

"Oh my. Seems I'm in a bit of trouble here, dear boy. Do you mind taking care of my camel for a little while?"

I took the rope from Simon as he was dragged to help Jesus. I led the camel along the outside of the crowd, following Jesus as closely as possible.

I heard Simon speak with Jesus as he strained under the weight of the beam. "I've heard of you, Jesus, and I believe your words are true. You are an innocent man, and it's an honor to carry this crossbeam for you. I only wish it did not have to be carried at all."

Jesus did not respond. He was forced to his feet and shoved forward to the top of the hill.

People lined both sides of the path up the hill. They spat on Jesus and threw rocks at him. Several of the rocks hit Simon as well.

"Kill the African!" some shouted. "Save a cross for him!"

"Thank you, Simon," Jesus said softly.

"As I said, it's an honor. Besides, now is no time for you to have to remember your manners. Something awful awaits you up ahead."

I looked up on hearing Simon's words. The top of Golgotha was bare except for Roman soldiers and rocks. There was not a tree or bush in sight. In just a few minutes the empty hill would be a place of death.

Read Luke 23:26

Lord, teach me how to take up my cross and follow you. Teach me how important it is to do what you ask, even if it's very difficult. Jesus, what you did for me was more difficult than I can imagine, and I thank you. Amen.

MEDITATION 35
HE HAD TO DIE

I did not climb Golgotha alone. The mob of people who hated Jesus grew larger, but I soon met up with many people who loved him. Mary, Martha, and Lazarus were among them. We climbed the hill together, crying quietly.

When we arrived at the top of the hill, we watched the soldiers make preparations. Simon dropped off the crossbeam and retrieved his camel from me.

"Thank you, son," he said. "I'm sorry I had to help the soldiers. Your friend does not deserve this."

We watched as the soldiers made their preparations. They took the crossbeam that Simon had carried and laid it on the ground. Then they laid Jesus down on the crossbeam and stretched his arms across it. Several of the soldiers made a game of spitting at Jesus as they worked.

I watched in horror as one soldier picked up several large spikes and a hammer. He walked to one of Jesus' hands and held it on the beam. I turned my head away. Then I heard the sound of metal as the hammer hit the spike.

Clang!

Clang!

Clang!

I clung to Mary Magdalene and cried. "How could they do this? How could God let this happen?" My knees became weak and I slid to the ground. Mary took me in her arms.

"Jesse," Mary said, "Jesus knew this would happen. It had to be this way. Everything is happening the way he said it would." She cried too. After a minute, she wiped her tears and spoke to me again. "That's why I poured out my perfume on him. Do you remember?"

I nodded my head but didn't look up.

"He always told us he would die, but no one believed him. And no one believed John the Baptist when he said Jesus was the Lamb who would take away our sin. You know what happens to lambs, don't you Jesse? They die to pay the price for other people's sins."

I nodded again and looked up at Mary. "I know," I said. "But why do the soldiers have to be so cruel?"

Mary did not answer me. She held my face close to her and looked up at Jesus. The soldiers had lifted him up and were securing the crossbeam to another beam that stood straight up from the ground.

I did not look up at Jesus until I heard him speak. His body and face were horrible to see, but his words told me everything was all right.

"Father," he said as he looked at the people around him. "Forgive them. They don't know what they're doing."

Only Jesus could have spoken those words. Only Jesus could have looked at the Roman soldiers and forgiven them.

The soldiers ignored Jesus. They put away their tools quietly. Then one of the soldiers saw the robe Martha had made for Jesus.

"Hey, what's this? It's Jesus' robe! He won't be needing this any longer. I say we split it up," he said.

"No, you idiot!" another one said. "This is fine material. You can't just tear it up. I say we throw dice for it—winner takes the robe!"

A small group had gathered around the soldiers to see who would win the robe. It didn't take long. The winner grabbed the robe and flung it in the air when he won.

"It's mine, O king of the Jews," he yelled at Jesus as he put on the robe. He paraded around the foot of the cross.

Some in the crowd joined the soldier in mocking Jesus.

"Save yourself, O king," they cried out and laughed. "You came to save others, why not save yourself?"

What angered me most was the way people made fun of Jesus as he died. I couldn't stand it any longer.

"No!" I yelled, running to the foot of the cross. "Get away! Get away!" I grabbed the robe from the Roman soldier and swung it in the air like a whip. He *is* the King! He's the Son of God! Get away!"

Soon I became dizzy from swinging the robe in circles and fell against the bottom of Jesus' cross. A Roman soldier grabbed the robe away from me and shoved me with his boot. "Beat it, you runt!" he said roughly. "You're lucky you're too young to be thrown in jail."

Lazarus ran forward and helped me up. "Come, Jesse. It will be all right. Let's go."

We stepped away from the cross, but I couldn't keep my tears back. These people didn't understand—I loved Jesus. I belonged to him. For the first time in my life, I had belonged to someone!

Read Luke 23:27-38

Lord, you died on the cross to save me from my sin. I thank you because now I can belong to you forever. Amen.

MEDITATION 36
THE CURTAIN FALLS

I looked up at Jesus as he hung on the cross. His form stood out against the bright blue sky. The heat of the sun beat down on the hill, and it seemed to make Jesus all the more miserable.

All at once, the sky went dark! It was like someone had thrown a black cloak over the sun. People around us panicked at the strange event. They shouted in surprise and tried to find their way down the hill in the darkness. I held onto Lazarus tightly.

"Don't worry Jesse. This may be God's way of easing the pain for Jesus. Perhaps he can die peacefully now, without the sun beating down or people looking at him."

I hoped Lazarus was right, but Jesus groaned all the more loudly and sadly. I covered my ears tightly to block out the sound.

My eyes adjusted to the darkness as people in the city lit candles and torches. In the distance I saw the roof of the temple. Lights glowed from beneath the tall gate.

As I stared at the temple, fresh anger boiled inside me. I pictured Jesus teaching there just a day ago. Yesterday Jesus was loved by all the people. Today he was hanging on a cross behind me.

Jesus himself had said he would die for the sins of the people, but somehow I couldn't understand what that meant for *me*. I decided to leave the hill and seek my answer in the temple. If the temple was the house of God, I could ask my questions there, and God would answer me.

I knew Lazarus would never let me go if I told him my plan.

"Lazarus," I asked, "may I go back to the city?"

"It's all right, Lazarus," Mary broke in. "The boy doesn't need to stay here and watch Jesus die this way. Let him go."

Before Lazarus could disagree, I ran down the hill and through the city gate. From there I followed the glow of the temple's lights. Within minutes I was standing in the courtyard.

"I must go farther in," I thought. "All the priests go in the temple to present sacrifices. That's where they meet God. That's where I must go."

It wouldn't be easy. There were temple guards everywhere. And everyone knew that if you entered the Most Holy Place of the temple you would die. I knew it was dangerous, but how else could I get an answer to my question? I was determined to risk it.

Even though there were many guards and priests, I found it easy to make my way through the temple. There were tall columns everywhere, and the shadows hid me from view. I crept through the outer courts and hid behind the altar of sacrifice until a priest passed by. As I turned, I saw steps leading up to the Holy Place. Beyond that was my goal—the Most Holy Place.

A tall curtain hung across the Most Holy Place so that no one could see inside. The curtain was said to separate God from people. Only the high priest was allowed behind the curtain, and even he could go there only once a year.

I looked from side to side. There were no priests in sight. I leaped from my hiding place and ran up the steps. But before I got halfway up, I was knocked off my feet.

The ground started to shake under me. "Earthquake!" I yelled. I fell down to the ground, grabbing for something to hold onto, but there was nothing there. I rolled to the bottom of the steps and looked up.

There in the glow of the lamps stood the curtain. Suddenly, I heard a tearing sound that was as loud as the earthquake. Dust flew from the curtain as the fabric ripped inch by inch. It was as if someone had grabbed the giant curtain with his hands and was splitting the fabric apart. Within seconds, the curtain was completely torn and fell in a heap to the floor.

I had the answer that I was looking for. There in front of me was the Most Holy Place. The place of God. It was once hidden by a curtain, but no more. Jesus had died, and I was sure that God would no longer be kept hidden behind the curtain. Jesus had died so that I could see God.

Read Luke 23:44-45

Lord, I praise you that you are with me now, and that I can look forward to being with you forever. I can't wait to see you face to face. I have a lot of questions to ask you, but most of all I just want to be with you. Amen.

MEDITATION 37

HE LOVED YOU, PETER

I sat there, staring at the torn curtain. It laid on a heap on the floor. But then I heard the sounds of men's voices. They were coming my way! They must have heard the sound of the curtain being torn. I quickly hid behind a large column that stood by a wall.

I was bursting to tell Lazarus and the others about the wonderful sign from God that I had seen! But the priests and guards took a long time to cover up the Most Holy Place. After they finished, my escape was simple. And when I stepped into the outer courts, the bright sunshine had returned.

As I walked through the temple gates, I heard several people talking excitedly about the sudden darkness and the earthquake. I wanted to stop and tell them that those were signs that surrounded Jesus' death, because he was the Son of God. I wanted to tell them that Jesus died to save us from our sin.

Just then, Lazarus grabbed me by the shoulder.

"Jesse! Are you all right? Where have you been? Mary, Martha, and I have been looking all over the city for you!"

I apologized. "I'm sorry, but listen! The temple curtain—it's down. It split in two from top to bottom. I saw inside the Most Holy Place!"

Lazarus did not believe me. "Listen, Jesse. No one's allowed in that far, especially a thirteen-year-old boy. Maybe you fell during the earthquake and dreamt it."

"No, Lazarus. Honest, I saw it! Come with me into the temple and see for yourself."

Lazarus thought for a moment. "It may be as you say. If it's true, then it must be a wonderful sign from God. But right now I think we should go back up the hill to see what we can do about Jesus. I have a feeling he's dead. We'll need to bury him before the sun goes down. Better for us to bury him than those awful Roman soldiers."

"But where will we bury him?"

"I've heard there's a member of the council who didn't agree with the decision to kill Jesus. He said he'd find a place for him. We can help take Jesus' body to the tomb."

I gave up trying to convince Lazarus about the curtain. We turned toward the city gate and made our way back up the hill to the crosses.

Everything was just as it had been when I left. Three crosses stood in

the ground. The criminals and Jesus still hung there. Jesus did not move or groan.

"Is he dead?" I asked Lazarus as we got closer.

"I think so, Jesse. Does it frighten you?"

"No it doesn't. And I'm not mad either. Mary was right. He had to die. And I saw why."

We approached the others around the cross. Everyone was there. Even Peter.

I leaped for joy at seeing Peter. I had worried about him ever since he had left crying from the courtyard where he denied Jesus.

"Peter," I cried out softly. I ran to him and hugged him tightly. He held me, too, but he did not speak. He could only stare at Jesus. Tears were streaming down Peter's face, but he didn't make a sound.

"It's OK, Peter," I said. "It's OK. Everything has happened just as Jesus said. He had to die."

Peter nodded his head. He knew I was right. But that was not why he was crying. He was still thinking about how he had denied Jesus. I could tell that the awful words he had spoken still hurt him very much.

"He loved you, Peter," I said.

"Yes, I know. And he loved you too, Jesse."

Read Luke 23:46-49

Lord, I want to praise you for loving me no matter what I'm like. You died so that I could enjoy your love. I'm sorry I caused you so much pain on the cross. Thank you for forgiving me. Amen.

MEDITATION 38

HE'S ALIVE!

"He's alive! He's alive!" Mary Magdalene shouted as she burst through the door.

"What do you mean, he's alive? Who are you talking about?" Levi asked.

"The Rabbi! The Master! Jesus! He's risen from the dead!"

"It's true, everyone!" Jesus' mother Mary interrupted. "We went to the tomb this morning. When we arrived, the stone was rolled away. And instead of guards, we found two angels. They said Jesus wasn't there."

The disciples could not believe the women. They thought the women were making up the story because they *wanted* to believe that Jesus was alive. And so they argued back and forth.

Peter paced the floor as the argument continued. Finally he grew tired of the yelling. He walked to the center of the room and raised his hand.

"I'm going to the tomb. I have to see for myself. The women may be right or they may be wrong. But we'll never know by staying here."

"I want to come with you," I said.

Peter nodded his head. "I'm going to run fast, so you'd better keep up."

"No problem," I said. "I'm not a kid anymore."

I was just as anxious as Peter was to find out if the women were telling the truth. Seeing the dark sky, feeling the earthquake, and watching the temple curtain split in two convinced me that anything could happen.

And I remembered Jesus' words: "I will rise again."

The words filled my legs with strength, and my heart pumped faster. When I arrived at the tomb, Peter had just entered. I waited outside. I was excited to see if the report was true, but I was still frightened at the thought of looking inside a tomb.

Peter didn't stay in the tomb very long. He bolted out, shouting, "He's gone! It's true!" He had a worried look on his face.

"Really? Are you sure?"

"Of course I'm sure. Come and see for yourself." He took me by the hand. "The linen they used to wrap the body—it's just lying there. See?"

"But does that mean he's alive?" I asked.

Peter threw up his hands. "I don't know. All I know is that his body isn't there. Let's go. We'll report to the others. Maybe they've heard something more by now."

We returned to the inn where the disciples were staying. The women were still there, and everyone was eager to hear our report.

"Well?" James asked. "Is it true?"

"It's true. Jesus isn't there."

"Did you see the angels?" Mary asked.

"No. No angels."

"But he *must* be alive. He said he would live again on the third day!"

"But there could be another explanation."

The talking went on for quite a while this way. The women were getting angry at the men for being so stubborn, and the men were angry with the women for being so excited. It wasn't until Andrew and Bartholomew burst through the door that the argument was settled.

"We saw him! We saw him!" Andrew shouted. The two disciples had left the day before to tell some friends what had happened to Jesus.

"We were walking down the road when a man caught up with us. We got to talking about Jesus' death. He explained the whole thing to us from the Scriptures. When we sat down for supper with him he broke the bread. Then we realized who he was. As soon as I yelled out "Jesus!," he disappeared. I tell you it was him. He's alive!"

The women stepped forward. Now they were certain Peter and the others would believe them. "Peter, we saw the angels and the empty tomb. You saw the empty tomb, too. These disciples saw Jesus himself. What's more, Jesus told us that he would rise from the dead. What more do you want?"

Levi answered for Peter. "To see him here in front of us, that's what!"

No sooner had Levi finished his sentence than Jesus appeared!

"It's a ghost!" Levi cried out. Several of the other disciples moved further back in the room.

"I'm not a ghost," Jesus said. "Why do you doubt that it is really me? Look at my hands and feet. Do ghosts have scars from wounds?"

Jesus stepped forward. My eyes met his as he looked around the room. Then I knew he was no ghost. It was Jesus!

I ran and threw my arms around him. I felt the warmth of his body. I smelled the fresh air in his clothes. This was no ghost. This was my Jesus!

Read Luke 24:1-12

Lord, you rose from the dead! Wow! You rose again so that when we die, we can go to heaven. I believe that you rose from the dead and that I'll see you again someday. Thank you, Jesus! Amen.

MEDITATION 39

HE'S IN HEAVEN!

Jesus stayed with us from that day on. He explained everything.

"You didn't always understand things when I was with you. You should have trusted me more. Let me tell you why things had to happen as I said. Do you remember what the prophet Isaiah said about the lamb?"

John answered. "Isaiah said he would be led to death without any argument, and that men would hate him."

"That's right. And why did Isaiah say that this would happen?"

"So the lamb could take the sins of many people on himself," Peter answered.

James added, "Isaiah said that you would be pierced for our sins too, didn't he?"

"You're right, all of you. And how about my returning to you? Do you remember that David said my body would not be left in the grave?"

Everyone nodded in agreement. Every boy in Israel had learned such lessons by heart. But it was not until Jesus explained these things that we understood.

We ate dinner together that night. Jesus also ate, and enjoyed being with his disciples again.

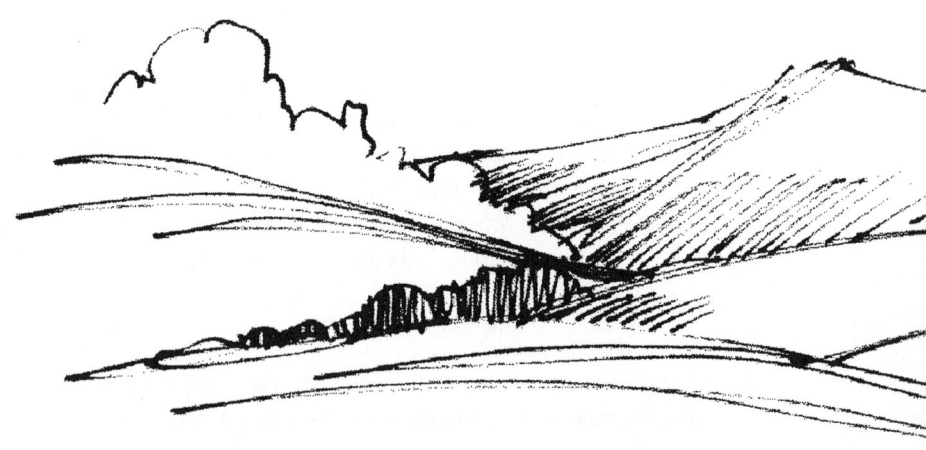

"I will be leaving you again soon," Jesus said. "But this time I won't die. I will be going to heaven to be with my Father. After that you will tell everyone what's happened, and how I came to save sinners. But you can't do that until after you've stayed in Jerusalem for a while. Do you understand?"

Everyone nodded. As I looked at Jesus' face, I saw a funny smile. It was as if he had some wonderful surprise in store for us.

We spent happy days walking throughout the countryside. As we traveled, many people saw that Jesus had truly risen. Then we went back down to Bethany. We stayed at the home of Mary and Martha, remembering and laughing about the times we had together.

I could not imagine living without Jesus, but the morning came when he said goodbye.

"Gentlemen," he woke us. "It's time to go!" Jesus' loud voice echoed inside the small room.

We set aside our blankets. The sun had already risen. The time had come, it seemed, for Jesus to really leave us. I could tell by the excitement in Jesus' voice. I felt like crying, but I held back my tears.

We traveled up the hill overlooking Jerusalem. There were no clouds in the sky. The rooftops of the city shone like gold in the bright sunshine. It was a beautiful sight.

Arriving at the top of the hill, Jesus turned to face us.

"I've loved having you as my disciples," he said. "You are not just my disciples. You are my friends. You are my brothers. I told you once before that I am going to prepare a place for you in heaven with my Father. You will rule with me someday. And then you will see my kingdom and be rewarded for your service to me. But remember, you are to serve one another. The least of you will be the greatest."

I remembered when Jesus used me to teach the disciples about being the greatest. I was proud then to be chosen. Now it didn't matter. "I just want to be with him," I thought. I gazed into his eyes.

"You will face many troubles on earth, but I will be with you. I will send the Holy Spirit to comfort and guide you. The Spirit will be your greatest blessing."

While he told us this, the air around us changed. A cloud appeared from nowhere, and Jesus' body was lifted into the sky by the cloud.

We all stood looking up, trying to spot him in the sky. He was gone. "Do you see him, Peter?" someone asked.

"No, I don't see a thing."

"Keep looking. Maybe he'll come back into view."

Suddenly, two men dressed in white robes were standing beside us. I jumped back. One of the men spoke:

"Why are you still looking up into the sky? He's gone. But he will come back in the same way that he left. Go back now, just as he commanded you, and wait in Jerusalem."

"Wait for what?" Peter asked.

"You'll see. Just go and wait." With that the two men disappeared.

John broke out in laughter. "Can you believe it? This is incredible! Let's hurry up and go. Jesus is alive and in heaven, and we saw it happen!"

As we turned to go back to Jerusalem, we started singing: "He's alive! He's alive! The Messiah is alive! Hallelujah, the Messiah is alive!"

Read Luke 24:50-53

Lord, thank you for going back to heaven to be with God. You promised to come back, and I can't wait to see you. Until then, teach me what you want me to do, and let me know that the Holy Spirit will help me as I work for you every day. Amen.

MEDITATION 40

I'VE GOT A STORY TO TELL

We walked down the hillside with Mary, Martha, and Lazarus. Soon we entered the town of Bethany again.

"We'll stay here," Lazarus said. "Jesus told you men to go to Jerusalem. We'll report to everyone here what has happened."

The disciples realized that they might not be able to enjoy spending time with their friends in Bethany again. They hugged and kissed Mary, Martha, and Lazarus goodbye.

"Come, Jesse. Let's go to Jerusalem," Peter said.

For the first time since I started following Jesus, I stood still after such a command. Before, I had always jumped when someone said "Let's go." But I wasn't sure this time.

Peter questioned me. "What's the matter? Don't you want to come with us?"

"It's not that I don't want to. It's just that. . . ."

"Oh," Mary said. "You want to stay with us, is that it? Well, you're welcome here Jesse. We would love having another younger brother."

I had not thought of staying with Mary and the others. Her invitation made me feel good. For a moment I thought of what it would be like to have a real family. But I shook my head no.

"No, thank you. I would love to stay here. But I have to go back to Capernaum. That's where I belong. I want to be a disciple there. I want to tell the people of that city about Jesus."

Peter smiled and spread his arms wide to hug me. I ran into them. He nearly crushed me with his big bear hug!

"I have no doubt that you will be a good disciple, young man," Peter said as he smiled at me. "You *are* a good disciple. Go on. Go to Capernaum. But don't go alone. Lazarus, would you travel with him to be sure he arrives safely? And Martha, make the boy some food for the trip, would you please? He eats like a horse."

I said goodbye to all the disciples. They walked down the road toward Jerusalem while I stayed with Mary, Martha, and Lazarus for one more day.

Early the next morning, Lazarus and I set out for Capernaum, my home. The five-day journey seemed to go quickly. Each bend in the road brought back memories. On the last day of our trip, I turned to Lazarus.

"I'll be OK from here. You'll save some time if you turn back now."

"Are you sure?"

"Yes. I'm sure. I know these parts better than you. Thank you so much for keeping me company along the way." We hugged each other, and I began the last part of my trip alone.

Several hours later I was about to enter Capernaum when a small boy came to me.

"Please, can you give me a coin?"

I turned to the small beggar.

"I don't have any money. But I do have a little bit of food here. And something else, too."

"What's that?" the boy asked eagerly.

"I have a story to tell you. A true story about a person named Jesus. Come, follow me and I'll tell you. I'll tell you everything."

Read Acts 1:4-8

Lord, I'm a disciple of yours. Show me the other people you want as disciples too. Teach me how to tell other people the good news about your love for us. Amen.